The Information Literacy Cookbook

CHANDOS
INFORMATION PROFESSIONAL SERIES

Series Editor: Ruth Rikowski
(email: Rikowskigr@aol.com)

Chandos' new series of books are aimed at the busy information professional. They have been specially commissioned to provide the reader with an authoritative view of current thinking. They are designed to provide easy-to-read and (most importantly) practical coverage of topics that are of interest to librarians and other information professionals. If you would like a full listing of current and forthcoming titles, please visit our web site **www.chandospublishing.com** or contact Hannah Grace-Williams on email info@chandospublishing.com or telephone number +44 (0) 1865 884447.

New authors: we are always pleased to receive ideas for new titles; if you would like to write a book for Chandos, please contact Dr Glyn Jones on email gjones@chandospublishing.com or telephone number +44 (0) 1865 884447.

Bulk orders: some organisations buy a number of copies of our books. If you are interested in doing this, we would be pleased to discuss a discount. Please contact Hannah Grace-Williams on email info@chandospublishing.com or telephone number +44 (0) 1865 884447.

The Information Literacy Cookbook

Cookbook

Ingredients, Recipes and Tips for Success

by:

JANE SECKER, DEBBI BODEN
AND GWYNETH PRICE

Chandos Publishing
Oxford · England

Chandos Publishing (Oxford) Limited
Chandos House
5 & 6 Steadys Lane
Stanton Harcourt
Oxford OX29 5RL
UK
Tel: +44 (0) 1865 884447 Fax: +44 (0) 1865 884448
Email: info@chandospublishing.com
www.chandospublishing.com

First published in Great Britain in 2007

ISBN:
978 1 84334 225 0 (paperback)
978 1 84334 226 7 (hardback)

1 84334 225 1 (paperback)
1 84334 226 X (hardback)

© Jane Secker, Debbi Boden and Gwyneth Price, 2007

British Library Cataloguing-in-Publication Data.
A catalogue record for this book is available from the British Library.

The Publishers make no representation, express or implied, with regard to the accuracy of the information contained in this publication and cannot accept any legal responsibility or liability for any errors or omissions.

The material contained in this publication constitutes general guidelines only and does not represent to be advice on any particular matter. No reader or purchaser should act on the basis of material contained in this publication without first taking professional advice appropriate to their particular circumstances.

Typeset by Avocet Typeset, Chilton, Aylesbury, Bucks.
Printed in the UK and USA.

Contents

Acknowledgements

We would like to thank everyone who has helped make this book possible; including all the hard working and enthusiastic contributors, who picked up and ran with the cookbook theme. We would also particularly like to thank Glyn Jones at Chandos for his patience and encouragement, and to Gareth Haman, our copy editor. We would like to thank Toby Bainton from SCONUL for permission to reproduce the SCONUL Seven pillars model of information literacy on page 126. Many people have helped make this book possible, but we'd particularly like to thank our employers for their support and patience and our friends and family. We'd also particularly like to thank Andrew and Tim for their support, and Tabitha Boden for the IL cookbook cartoons! Thanks also to Chris Fryer and Steve Bond for their help with photos and images. Last but not least, we'd like to thank each other for the mutual support and friendship we have enjoyed throughout the project.

Introducing the chefs: about the authors

Debbi Boden

Debbi Boden is a Faculty Team Leader at Imperial College London. She is chair of the Library Online Information Literacy Group and leads on the College's information literacy (IL) programmes for students, academic and library staff. Debbi is also Chair and founder of the CILIP CSG Information Literacy Group, whose aim is to promote IL across all sectors, and who organises the Librarian Information Literacy Annual Conference (LILAC). Debbi is currently working with the Bradford Metropolitan Council on a pilot project Pop-i. Pop-i is a unique collaboration between Higher Education and the Public sector to create an online programme to teach enquiry desk staff in public libraries about IL and to help them develop the skills to transfer that knowledge into the work place.

As someone who finds kitchens frightening, it is somewhat ironic that Debbi should be involved in the creation of a 'cookbook'! The best poster she ever saw said 'I only have a kitchen because it came with the house!'. A friend once introduced her and said, 'this is Debbi, she burns salad', and that really sums up the situation. Cook Debbi a meal and she will be forever grateful! So what are her favourite foods? A glass of cold crisp dry white wine and Lindt chocolate!

Gwyneth Price

Gwyneth Price works four days a week as Student Services Librarian at the Institute of Education, University of London. As well as being responsible for acquisition of books and other resources on reading lists, including the creation of electronic course packs, she works closely with academic staff and students to develop their information literacy. As an ex-school teacher, Gwyneth is very aware of the importance of information literacy education for teachers. In her 'spare' day, Gwyneth works freelance on a range of projects and is currently a Fellow of the Centre for Distance Education, University of London.

Gwyneth is something of a Grecophile, so her favourite recipes taste of the sun; ideally involving fresh fish and very simple ingredients like juicy tomatoes, basil and rocket, and delicious fresh bread. Failing that, something featuring chocolate, cherries and a dash of brandy would be just right for a winter evening.

Jane Secker

Jane Secker is Learning Technology Librarian at the Centre for Learning Technology, based at the London School of Economics. She advises staff about issues of copyright and licensing and coordinates an information literacy training programme for staff. Jane is Conference Officer for the CILIP Information Literacy Group that organises LILAC (Librarians' Information Literacy Annual Conference). Jane is also Chair of ALISS (Association of Librarians and Information professionals in the Social Sciences) and Chair of the Heron User Group. Jane has worked on a number of research projects, including the MIDESS (Management of Images in a Distributed Environment with Shared Services) project and DELIVER (Digital Electronic Library Integrating Virtual Learning EnviRonments) project, both funded by the Joint Information Systems Committee (JISC). She received her PhD from the University of Wales, Aberystwyth in 1999, which was a study of newspapers and historical research.

Jane loves cooking, eating and drinking, and as a non-meat eater her favourite recipe would probably be Italian influenced and include lots of fresh ingredients such as tomatoes, garlic, onions and cheese, for example home made pizza or spinach and ricotta cannelloni with a garlicky tomato sauce, served with bread and a green salad and all washed down with lashings of red wine!

Contributor biographies

Carey Craddock

Carey Craddock has worked as an information specialist at a Unilever research site since 1998 and has a number of different responsibilities. She is the sole trainer for the Information Group, is creating and delivering an information literacy programme, and is currently developing an e-learning tutorial. Carey is also an information scientist, undertaking literature searches and analyses for customers interested in new science areas.

Prior to her job at Unilever she held a variety of information roles in local government and for a newspaper publishing company. In 1998 she gained a Library and Information Studies MA at Loughborough University. She is a chartered member of CILIP.

Carey's favourite food is Italian, so any dish which contains pasta, fish and garlic always goes down well. Eating out is her favourite way to enjoy food, preferably in an outdoor Mediterranean restaurant!

Jane Del-Pizzo

Jane worked as a learning resources centre manager for further education colleges in London between 2000 and 2005, including City and Islington College and Lewisham College. She is currently working for a legal education provider and finally utilising her drama training in recording podcasts for library tours and interactive guides to legal research. In her spare time she enjoys knitting, adventure travel and hosting backpackers, in addition to keeping ferrets.

Cooking likes include anything with chocolate in – Jane's specialities include boozy desserts, although these aren't recommended for the 16–19 year age group!

Angela Donnelly

Angela Donnelly has worked in the Information Centre for Unilever R&D, Port Sunlight, since 1997. She works in a global team and delivers a training/education programme and provides access to relevant databases and tools as well as other traditional library services.

She has a first class honours degree in Information and Library Studies from Liverpool John Moores University and also has experience of working in an HE Library as well as in the NHS.

Originally from South Africa, Angela particularly enjoys any cooking that involves being outdoors, weather permitting, so her favourite recipes are for BBQs.

Sarah Hinton

Sarah Hinton began her career in regional government libraries with the Department of Environment and Ministry of Defence. She joined Scientific Generics (now called Sagentia) in the solo position of Corporate Librarian in 1995. In 2004, she joined Manage5Nines Ltd., a new company formed from the (previously internal) Scientific Generics information technology (IT) and information services. As part of Manage5Nines, Sarah has been able to expand her client base and provides business information services to other companies, as well as remaining corporate librarian for the Sagentia Group. She is a chartered member of CILIP and member of the SLA.

Sarah enjoys cooking and trying out new recipes, especially when it includes using home-grown vegetables. But she is most happy with simple food, so a vegetable hotpot is hard to beat as her ideal meal, especially after a long cycle ride!

Rebecca Jones

Rebecca Jones has worked at Malvern St James (formerly Malvern Girls' College) since 1998. She was awarded her PhD from Loughborough University in 2001 and it was this research into the management implications of multimedia applications that started her interest in teaching and learning in relation to new technology.

Within schools she actively promotes information literacy and has been involved in developing skills-based lessons within the majority of subject areas across the different key stages. She works closely with teaching staff in both the planning and delivery of these sessions.

She has an active interest in her profession and is a committee member of both the School Libraries Group and the Information Literacy Group.

Rebecca enjoys eating cake, drinking hot chocolate and sampling the wide variety of baked items available at her local coffee shops and cafes. She likes traditional, home-cooked meals and, after many years, has realised that the flavour of most dishes is enhanced if someone else has cooked it.

Di Millen

Di Millen is the Head of Informatics at NHS Connecting for Health – the Department of Health Agency charged with delivery of the NHS National Programme for IT. Di has worked in the NHS for more than 25 years in a variety of management roles, and in information and IT education, training and development roles for the last 15 of these. Di introduced the European Computer Driving Licence (ECDL) as the national reference standard for basic IT skills into the NHS and continues to work towards the effective use of information and ICT by all 1.3 million NHS staff as a contributor to improvements in patient care.

Her culinary passion is for pasta and all that goes with it – garlic bread, olives, basil and fresh parmesan, washed down with a large glass of (probably New World) red wine!

Rónán O'Beirne

Ronan O'Beirne has recently taken up the post of Assistant Director for Learning Development at Bradford College in West Yorkshire. He has over 20 years' experience of working and developing learning services in public libraries; in his previous post as Principal Libraries Officer for Information and Learning at City of Bradford Public Libraries he set up an innovative learning zone. He has pioneered the development of community networking and online learning initiatives and has acted as a consultant to BECTa, the DfES, University for Industry and the European Union. In collaboration with Imperial College London, he has developed and delivered a unique information literacy e-learning programme within public libraries – he hopes to extend this into the Further Education sector.

In his spare time Ronan grows a varied range of organic fruit and vegetables on his allotment holding by the river Aire in Bingley. He enjoys cooking with fresh ingredients and trying out different combinations of taste.

Helen Roberts

Helen Roberts has worked in the NHS since May 2002 after working in various IT Support/Technical roles in the private sector. Helen is currently the IT Training, Support and Projects Team Leader, with the additional role of Test Centre Manager for ECDL. Helen has also completed various Adult and Further Education Teacher Training including CertEd and is a Certified TAP Trainer with the Institute of IT Training. Helen is also involved in numerous NHS Connecting for Health Education, Training and Development Initiatives and Projects.

Helen enjoys cooking and entertaining, recently creating a monthly 'cook off' as an excuse to get together with some of her best friends. The nights are generally filled with very good food, a few good tipples, a couple of score sheets, and a healthy competitive nature!

Appetisers and aperitifs: getting started with the information literacy cookbook

Jane Secker, Debbi Boden and Gwyneth Price

How to read this book

The Information Literacy Cookbook is something different. It's not a book to read from cover to cover. It's a book to take with you into the 'kitchen'. A book to balance your coffee cup on. A book to spill flour, milk and many other ingredients on. Most of all it is a book to keep by your side, to dip into regularly. It's a book to turn to when you need inspiration, or advice. It's very much written *by* practitioners *for* practitioners, and we make no apologies about this. All three editors of this book are library practitioners in higher education (HE), so we are well aware of how information literacy (IL) affects people's ability not just to learn, but to go about their day-to-day lives. However, as librarians we recognise that providing access to information is only the first part of the process. Knowing how to interpret, analyse and use information in an ethical manner is vital if we are to transform people's ability to learn and thrive in the digital world.

IL, however, is no longer just an HE affair it is something that is crucial to all aspects of our lives in the twenty-first century and its needs must be addressed in all areas of life. We are already starting to see a widening gap between the digitally advantaged and the digitally disadvantaged, those who have access to IT, ICT and IL training and those who do not. IL empowers people so they can make informed decisions, otherwise they become disenfranchised, and we as librarians have a key role to play in this arena. It is an issue that we have only just tapped the surface of, and is far bigger than perhaps we realise:

> Information Literacy is more than a library or education issue. It is crucial to issues of economic development, health, citizenship and quality of life. (Douglas, 2006)

In writing this book, the editors wanted to create something that would be of day-to-day use to practitioners; both experienced librarians and those who are new to teaching and learning in libraries. But why a 'cookbook', you may ask? Cookbooks come in different shapes and forms, but ultimately they are there to provide you with practical guidance, inspiration and ideas. They suggest new ways to enliven a traditional dish, or tips for using up store cupboard ingredients. Cookbooks can be followed step-by-step by the amateur, or used as a springboard for the experienced chef. A good cookbook is colourful and bursting with mouthwatering flavours and it tempts you to get off the sofa and into the kitchen! We hope that this cookbook will be both practical and inspiring; combining the best of new technologies and traditional tried and tested methods. They say that 'too many cooks spoil the broth', yet we believe that variety is the spice of life. That's why we've brought together experts from across the library and information sectors to author each chapter. You'll find each chapter examines a different sector in the library world and we hope you find this variety both lively and inspiring. And as with a cookbook we hope you won't just read the section on meat or fish, but you'll dip into the other chapters that offer new perspectives. Hence we encourage HE librarians to read the public libraries chapter, and for those in the commercial sector to read about what's happening in schools. But whatever you do, enjoy yourself, don't be afraid to experiment, and if all else fails you can always turn to some of our tried and tested recipes.

A little bit of background

If you are new to the concept of information literacy, you may find it helpful to explore some of the definitions. Professional bodies in the US, Australia and UK have established definitions of the term and overviews of these are available in a variety of publications (Bawden, 2001; Virkus, 2003) and from the Information Literacy website (*http://www.informationliteracy.org.uk*). However, IL has become a global issue and international groups such as UNESCO are working together to look at ways of moving the IL agenda forward worldwide:

> UNESCO's action to provide people with the skills and abilities for critical reception, assessment and use of information in their professional and personal lives. (UNESCO, 2005)

The Alexandria Proclamation provided another landmark in the realisation of the importance of IL when it stated that:

> Information Literacy lies at the core of lifelong learning ... Life long learning enables individuals, communities and nations to attain their goals and to take advantage of emerging opportunities in the evolving global environment for shared benefit. It assists them and their institutions to meet technological, economic and social challenges, to redress disadvantage and to advance the well being of all. (IFLA, 2005)

For the purposes of this book the authors have used CILIP's (The Chartered Institute of Library Information Professionals) IL definition:

> IL is knowing when and why you need information, where to find it, and how to evaluate, use and communicate it in an ethical manner. (CILIP, 2004)

The remit of those involved in the creation of the definition was to provide something in simple language that could be adapted depending on sector or audience (Armstrong et al., 2005). The use of it in this book demonstrates that it acts as a springboard for the development of IL programmes across all sectors. The January/February 2005 issue of *CILIP Update* was a special issue devoted to information literacy and was an important signal that IL had arrived in the UK (CILIP, 2005).

The term 'information literacy' has been challenged by many, and alternative terms are frequently discussed, but the continuing debate about definitions diverts attention from the need to make IL a reality. As one author argues:

> The literature on information literacy reveals the presence of a consensual core that has developed as a result of a multitude of contributions towards the delineation of the concept ... That so much controversy still exists regarding the term is not for a lack of a clear definition but the absence of a clear line of action and the will and practical chance to implement it. (Owusa-Ansah, 2003)

It is clear that definitions of IL are difficult to translate into real life situations and we wanted to find ways to describe IL via metaphors or analogies. Cooking was something that seemed to fit. Our discussions and reflections initially saw parallels with Jamie Oliver's work with school meals, the idea of recipe ingredients as 'keywords', quick snacks, fast food, pick and mix, full scale a la carte menus; the analogies are endless. Indeed a recent debate on the British discussion list *LIS-Infoliteracy* tackled the question of whether we are over-egging the pudding. And the response has to be that the proof of the pudding is in the eating: are libraries making a difference?

In writing this book the editors recognise that the library profession has changed enormously in the last 5 to 10 years, largely due to the rapid developments in information and communication technologies. The Internet has dramatically increased the range of information available and the way in which it is delivered. With the rise of the Internet and web technology there can be no doubting that access to information has improved. Nevertheless, to assume that because information is available on the web, people will have the skills and knowledge to find, access and use it effectively is naive. As Laurillard said:

> It is as absurd to try and solve the problems of education by giving people access to information as it would be to solve the

housing problem by giving people access to bricks. (Laurillard, 2002).

A recently published book edited by Levy and Roberts (2005), *Developing the New Learning Environment: the Changing Role of the Academic Librarian*, clearly describes the impact of changes in higher education on the role of the academic librarian. However, we must also recognise that underlying the changes in education are more fundamental changes that have occurred in society in the last 10 years driven by changes in information and communications technologies (ICTs). Some librarians, especially in HE, are well prepared for their role in an IT rich environment, but this is not true across all sectors. As electronic access has increased, the need for 'user education' has become more apparent. As Phil Bradley has demonstrated, the development of CD-ROM technology forced academic librarians to recognise the learning needs of students (Bradley, 2006).

Judith Peacock's (in Levy and Roberts, 2005) offers a rallying cry from the Australian perspective, examining 'information literacy education in practice'. Describing the current battle over teaching and learning between pedagogists and technologists, she sees librarians as holding 'an enviable position in the conflict' (Levy and Roberts, 2005; p. 154). Peacock argues that information literacy is crucial and, citing Alan Bundy, maintains that 'in a teaching world gone technologically mad, librarians can provide a balanced and discriminating view of the place of ICT in education'. She illustrates her points with a case study from Queensland University of Technology, but is clear that 'it is not enough ... to stand out and challenge old paradigms; they [librarians] must offer solutions and create new perceptions of information literacy education' (Levy and Roberts, 2005; p. 177). While this role may be increasingly secure in the HE sector, librarians in other types of libraries have other hurdles still to overcome. Public libraries have no consistent 'audience' and work at the Enquiry Desk or through online support will have to suffice. Similarly, in many workplace libraries there is still an expectation that the Library will provide information (or even knowledge) but not necessarily the competence to find it. Public libraries have no consistent 'audience' and yet, with the government's commitment to the 'e-agenda', their role becomes increasingly important. The term 'digital citizenship' has come into being but do people really understand what it means?

Activity in IL suggests that we are moving on and that the concept of IL is becoming embedded in the vocabulary of education and learning. For example, alongside the many references to IL in library and information studies journals and conference proceedings, there is increased reference and understanding in mainstream academic writing and in the public domain. As access to technology grows, the obvious failure to find and evaluate resources becomes more apparent and educators are recognising the need for appropriate intervention. At the same time the so-called 'digital natives' are growing in confidence that 'Googling' will suffice. Librarians need more than their traditional searching skills, they need to be able to teach their patrons how to find and evaluate appropriate resources. In the face of Google librarians also need to demonstrate their continuing importance in the information supply chain. Yes Google is good, but Jasco (cited in Miller and Peller, 2006) has likened its approach to 'mixing in a gigantic bowl the appetiser, soup, entree, salad, dessert and coffee'. You may get the right ingredients, but what discerning diner wants to combine their salad and their coffee? And how do you taste the soup when it's mixed in with your dessert?

In response to this need librarians are focusing on two strands of development: helping library staff to develop their own IT and information literacy, and providing appropriate training opportunities for librarians to learn to teach. Specific courses are available through CILIP and its various groups, through local consortia, such as cpd25 in London and south-east England, through MLA in its *Inspiring Learning for All* strategy and in Health Authorities. Courses previously only open to lecturers in FE and HE are increasingly more welcoming and appropriate to learning support staff and the Higher Education Academy (HEA) also welcomes librarians.

In addition, a growing number of weblogs (blogs) focus on information literacy and some provide practical ideas on how to motivate and encourage learners. We hope that this book will provide a welcome addition to the kind of recipes that can be tried, modified and rewritten to suit the needs of individual teachers and learners and encourage sharing of ideas among practitioners.

Structure of the book

The book is divided into seven main chapters. Each chapter is written by a different author or authors and provides a recipe for success in a different sector of the library profession. Rather like a recipe book might have a chapter on fish dishes, a chapter on meat dishes, a chapter on vegetables and a chapter on pasta and rice dishes, this book looks at information literacy from the perspective of professionals in seven major sectors.

Chapter 2 starts by thinking of information literacy as widely as possible and what greater challenge is there for our public librarians than to meet the needs of the masses, or for that matter whoever walks through their door. Rónán O'Beirne is a former Principal Librarian at Bradford City Library and provides a thought provoking and inspiring start to the book. He uses analogies between the allotments movement with the development of public libraries and argues that information literacy is not something new for those in the public sector. Helping ordinary people find and use information has always underpinned the heart of the public library movement and remains as relevant today with the move towards digital citizenship.

Healthy bodies and healthy minds go hand in hand and this is very much the theme in Chapter 3 that examines information literacy in the health sector. Di Millen and Helen Roberts explore the importance of IT literacy for staff in the health services as an essential prerequisite for the development of information literacy in our electronic world.

We next turn to information literacy in the commercial sector in Chapter 4. Angela Donnelly and Carey Craddock are information specialists from Unilever and present a view from a company that very much recognises the value of information literacy and the role for its library staff. While this company may be atypical, it certainly provides food for thought for others in this sector.

Chapter 5 is authored by Sarah Hinton, who looks at information literacy issues and the solo librarian. 'Alone in the Kitchen' discusses the skills needed to manage a busy information service and how to develop information literacy alongside the traditional role of providing essential information to busy professionals.

We move on to focus on information literacy in the Schools sector in Chapter 6: 'Educating the palate of pupils and teachers'. Rebecca Jones, who works at Malvern St James, explores models of information literacy education for students and strategies for developing IL awareness among staff. Her emphasis on developing a vision and sharing it is relevant to all sectors.

Chapter 7 examines IL in Further Education, which can be one of the most challenging sectors for information and library professionals. Gwyneth Price and Jane del-Pizzo describe strategies and practical tips for working in Colleges that may have students of all ages from 14 to 90+, studying anything from basic skills to degree level courses.

In Chapter 8, we finally examine information literacy and the Higher

Education sector. The placing of this chapter at the end of the book is significant, for many will argue that information literacy is purely an issue for Higher Education. We would argue that IL is something that underpins the work of everyone in the Library and Information profession.

We hope you find this book inspiring, useful but most of all fun to read. We hope to give you plenty of food for thought, new ideas to spice up your induction sessions, or something to add a little extra flavour to your regular teaching. So what are you waiting for? Put your apron on and let's get cooking!

The Editors (from left to right: Jane Secker, Gwyneth Price and Debbi Boden).

References

Armstrong, C., and colleagues from the Information Literacy Group (2005) 'Defining information literacy for the UK', *Library and Information Update*. Available at *http://www.cilip.org.uk/publications/updatemagazine/archive/archive2005/janfeb/armstrong.htm* (accessed 6 March 2007).

Bawden, D. (2001) 'Information and digital literacies: a review of concepts', *Journal of Documentation*, 57(2): 218–59.

Bradley, P.(2006) 'From CD to the internet'. Presentation to CILIP Library and Information History Group 'Computers in Libraries' conference, 9 November 2006. Available at *http://slideshare.net/gofull/7225/30* (accessed 3 February 2007).

CILIP (2004) Information literacy: definition. Available at *http://www.cilip.org.uk/professionalguidance/informationliteracy/definition/* (accessed 6 March 2007).

CILIP (2005) *Library and Information Update*. Jan/Feb.

Douglas, J. (2006) 'French military victories?', keynote paper for LILAC conference 2006. Available at *http://www.cilip.org.uk/NR/rdonlyres/84438AF5-E5A0-446F-BA69-CF6CC9188439/0/Douglas.ppt* (accessed 6 March 2007).

IFLA (2005) The Alexandria proclamation on information literacy and lifelong learning. Available at *http://www.ifla.org/III/wsis/BeaconInfSoc.html* (accessed 6 March 2007).

Laurillard, D. (2002), quoted in Big Blue Connect (2003) *Final Report*, JISC/Manchester Metropolitan University. Available at: *http://www.library.mmu.ac.uk/bbconnect/finalreport.html* (accessed 14 March 2007).

Levy, P. and Roberts, S. (2005) *Developing the New Learning Environment: the Changing Role of the Academic Librarian*. London: Facet Publishing.

Miller, W. and Peller, R.M. (eds) (2006) *Libraries and Google*. Binghamton, NY: Haworth Press.

Owusa-Ansah, E.K. (2003) 'Information literacy and the academic library: a critical look at a concept and the controversies surrounding it', *Journal of Academic Librarianship*, 29(4): 219–30.

UNESCO (2005) 'Capacity building'. Available at *http://portal.unesco.org/ci/en/ev.php-URL_ID=15886&URL_DO=DO_TOPIC&URL_SECTION=201.html* (accessed 6 March 2007).

Virkus, S. (2003) 'Information literacy in Europe: a literature review', *Information Research*, 8(4): paper no. 159. Available at *http://informationr.net/ir/8-4/paper159.html* (accessed 7 March 2007).

2

Feeding the masses: digital citizenship and the public library

Rónán O'Beirne

Introduction

The secret to good cooking lies in the use of fresh ingredients. Food historians will give you the logical explanations, tell you about the many accidents that occurred to make certain combinations and explain the origins of traditional diets and dishes. Food serves as a fitting backdrop to the development of many social activities. Whether it is expressed in the sudden changes to diet that took place during the industrial revolution and more extreme periods of famine, or the more gradual evolution in tandem with changes that take place within society such as the rise of pre-packaged meals, food tells many stories. While the social history of food is indeed very interesting and the history of cooking equally fascinating, the fact remains that in order to make a superb meal, as any good cook will tell you, what really matters, above all else, is the quality of the ingredients.

This chapter looks at the growing need for an information literacy (IL) approach within public libraries. It identifies three aspects of the public library service that are particularly suited to such an approach: general enquiry work, supporting lifelong learners and supporting digital citizenship.

The rise of the Public Library

The Allotments movement[1] came about in order to cater for the wish of the newly industrialised worker to retain some contact with the land and to harvest freshly-grown produce.

> When I comes home at night, my missus always has something ready for me out of the garden and I fancy my taturs and cabbage, and everything is so much sweeter and better off my own ground than if we'd go to buy 'em. (Razzell and Wainwright, 1973; p. 55. The quoted text is from a letter to the Morning Chronicle dated 26th December 1849)

The development of the allotments movement offers an interesting comparison with the public library movement. If the allotment movement put food in the bellies of the emerging industrial society, the public library fed its intellectual needs.

The public library movement can be seen as one of the greatest success stories of the last few centuries. As a free service it was born in the midst of an economic period that had a general need to educate the new urban masses. This growing population took those first tentative steps towards a new industrial society; a fledgling society that held much promise for those prepared to rely on their intellect alone rather than accept their place in the pre-ordained social order based solely on land ownership. The first seeds of today's knowledge society were planted in those early industrial days where the ability of the individual worker to follow complex written instructions, rather than rely on traditional processes handed down over generations, provided the impetus for rapid economic growth. Those first public libraries provided universal access, encouraging and supporting the principle of a literate and numerate society.[2]

By the middle of the twentieth century, the public library was accepted as a core service offered by a local authority. The 1964 Public Libraries and Museums Act embedded the service within the legislature. This had the dual effect of securing and protecting the public library while at the same time laying it at the mercy and vagaries of town-hall financial management and planning. Books, still relatively highly regarded, were seen not only as fulfilling an educational role, but also they supported a leisure need. However the inconsistent positioning of libraries in different directorates of local government betrayed the fact that a clear local vision led by libraries was a rarity. Librarians, finding themselves in leisure departments competing for resources shoulder to shoulder with managers of swimming pools and playing fields, extolled the virtues of reading for leisure. Their counterparts, positioned in education departments, highlighted the benefits of libraries to the overall education effort, in the hope that their services could gain favour and funding.

Certainly there has been longstanding recognition that formal learning, that is learning within schools, colleges and universities, is supported in many ways by public libraries. More interestingly, recently some have suggested the public library laid the foundations for informal learning. Noticeably, within the past 10 years, coinciding with the concept of lifelong learning, the public library has been a prime mover in many adult and community learning initiatives.

The mainstay of the library has always been the book; however, there has been a constant challenge to the librarian to adapt to advances in media formats. The competition for leisure time and the ubiquitous television has led the library to diversify into areas such as video and DVD rental. We can see a similarity with the allotment garden where, during the war years, every inch of space was used to support the growing of the highest yielding crops (Comedia, 1993).

Nowadays allotments have a more relaxed feel and are seen as less regimented, often experimenting with low-yield, more exotic crops. Within the more densely populated suburbs they, along with libraries, can be seen as a sanctuary or indeed a neutral and shared space within the community. In a similar vein, public libraries have diversified – with varying degrees of success. Those that have been successful have remained close to the needs of the communities they serve while at the same time embracing the ever-changing national agenda.

Because of its all-encompassing user base, throughout this treatment of the public library a more discursive approach has been taken rather than simply providing a series of unique recipes for transferring the knowledge and skills of information literacy. To put together an information literacy meal that whets the appetite of the typical user of a public library is an impossible task. The reason is quite simple: there is no such thing as a typical public library user and, by extension, there is immense diversity in the type of public library one can find across the UK. Indeed there have been repeated, and failed, attempts to standardise public libraries and to deliver a consistent service, yet the fact remains that the greatest quality a library can have is that it reflects and supports the range of qualities and values held by it users.

Starter: supporting reference and enquiry work

I would suggest that the starter has two requirements: to introduce the diner to the general tastes about to be discovered, and to take the edge off the diner's hunger or enhance their appetite.

Throughout the life of the public library, librarians and library users have placed a strong importance on reference and enquiry services. From the perspective of information literacy the enquiry desk is the focal point for most activity within the public library. Rarely does a day go by without there being some enquiry with which staff have grappled. Whether they have been successful or not is often less important than the process that has been undertaken.

The core reference collection is similar to the basic ingredients that are to be found in the kitchen of even the most modest cook. The dictionary, encyclopaedia and handbook provide the olive oil, wine vinegar and seasoning of the vinaigrette, used so often not only in the many starter dishes but also the side-salad dressing that frequently accompanies the main course. This core reference collection is often supplemented by other approaches such as user education programmes.

In recent years there has been an acceptance that in order to exploit the information and communications technology infrastructure, society needs to become information literate. The public library can offer a bountiful produce, yet in order to make this available either the library worker must act as custodian of the collection or the user is given unrestricted access and left to negotiate what is on offer. It is where the latter approach is taken that we see a greater need for information literacy. Most of us have greater confidence in a system that is transparent. Our food distribution system has evolved in a way that a large element of trust has been placed in supermarket retail. Items of food, a tin of black-eyed beans for instance, carry more 'metadata' than the average conference proceeding; country of origin, sell-by date, ingredients, nutritional values, allergy advice and even details of how best to dispose of the tin. The point is that consumers of foodstuffs are no different from consumers of information. It is possible to act on behalf of the information seeker provided the process is agreed, transparent and ultimately inclusive. But the days of the library worker performing magic, pulling a crucial citation from an upturned hat, have all but passed. We are now in a more enlightened era where enabling and encouraging the library user to seek for themselves is, quite rightly, seen as the best approach to sustaining the very existence of libraries. This passage taken from *The Name of the Rose* describes a monastic library; some of the attributes, perhaps to a lesser degree, may have characterised the approach of a few public libraries.

> The library was laid out on a plan which has remained obscure to all over the centuries, and which none of the monks is called upon to know. Only the librarian has received the secret, from the

librarian who preceded him, and he communicates it, while still alive, to the assistant librarian, so that death will not take him by surprise and rob the community of that knowledge. And the secret seals the lips of both men. Only the librarian has, in addition to that knowledge, the right to move through the labyrinth of books, he alone knows where to find them, and where to replace them, he alone is responsible for their safekeeping. (Eco, 1983)

It is within the reference library that the argument really takes shape. Historically there have been two movements in reference work: conservative and liberal. Conservative saw the need for the service user to be self-reliant and to fend for him or herself in the library; the librarian helped show how the tools of the trade were to be used, this essentially was user education. After this came the liberal approach; users became remote, telephones were used and librarians found it easier to answer the enquiries themselves. Librarians became the fountains of information sitting between the enquirer and the information, and they took great professional pride in this position. Then came the computer. Librarians, still cast in the role of mediators, embraced the computer and explored it uses, primarily carrying out online searches on behalf of users. In the early 1990s with the introduction of the graphical user interface (GUI) the obscure syntax of the online search string was exposed. The mouse arrived and sat on the librarian's desk. Files and directories were no longer just kept on shelves, they were now kept inside the computer. But that was just the beginning; then came the Internet. Then, the easy to use web-browser and the search engine and almost overnight the librarian was no longer in the middle. The user was going directly to the resource. The term disintermediation came to the fore and the role of the librarian yet again was in need of clear definition. (Fritch and Mandernack, 2001)

It is important to note that the empowerment of the end user and the disintermediation of information services, seen today as a good thing, came about not by any well thought-out policy but rather as a result of the impact of technological determinism on public libraries. The user, particularly with the introduction of the GUI, was handed the keys to the kitchen and its larder. The librarian, who had for years acted as quartermaster now appeared at best confused and at worst redundant. The library user, it was feared, had been let loose in the kitchen with a box of matches and the bottle of cooking sherry.

Information literacy then, within today's public library, should be seen as more than simply user education; it seeks to extend the benefits of disintermediation to the library worker and the user alike. It does this by empowering and encouraging the user to adopt the skills and principles of information management in order to exploit the resources in, and accessed through, the library, while at the same time it releases the library worker from the outdated role of custodian and provides for a more focused supporting role.

As a starter, supporting the information enquiry provides an excellent basis from which to build greater services. It prepares the tastebuds for something more and introduces a theme or a motif that is echoed in later courses.

Main course: supporting learners

We have seen how the early development of the public library movement took as its main impetus the support of the free educational ideal, the betterment of society and the raising of the status of the working classes. In today's society there exists a similar impetus. The concept of lifelong learning has been embraced by the European communities ever since Jacques Delors' identification of economic competitiveness as the solution to a sustained and thriving Europe (Delors, 1996).

The benefits of lifelong learning, in terms of the economic motive, have to a large degree become easily and quickly accepted. Its benefits as an empowering paradigm for the individual with the potential to provide greater citizenship has been accepted less quickly and, in some quarters, with suspicion.[3]

A growing body of research identifies how in current times public libraries are supporting learners. Proctor and Bartle, for example, although concerned with low achieving learners have gathered significant data, both quantitative and qualitative, relating to the use of public libraries for learning. Their key findings confirm the notion that there is a strong link between libraries and learning:

> Many respondents recalled how browsing the public library shelves had sparked their interest in a subject and this, in turn had led to formal learning. We believe browsing in a public library has not been sufficiently recognised as a powerful tool for encouraging learning both formal and informal. (Proctor and Bartle, 2002)

At a national policy level most recently the key strength of libraries is acknowledged as supporting informal learners.

Libraries allow informal individual learning, clubs and communities for learning (such as local history) as well as providing a range of short evening and daytime courses. (Department of Culture, Media and Sport, 2003)

The needs of informal learners, identified by Coffield (2000) are seen as particularly well catered for by public libraries and this is the area where libraries can have the greatest impact.

I can sit there and its like a wonderful bag of goodies. I'm trying to read all the old Derbyshire newspapers from 1785, and its superb – I know things the experts don't! When you're studying for qualifications you go in straight lines – now I wander. (Chesterfield library user; Proctor and Bartle, 2002)

This quote encapsulates much of the spirit of informal learning in public libraries.

Looking through the information literacy lens at the public library, we can clearly see that supporting lifelong learning shares some common ground with university and college libraries. However on closer inspection there is one outstanding and significant difference. The public library caters in the main for informal learners while institutions such as a university have a formal learning group. The significance lies in how difficult it is to transfer information literacy skills from staff to library users within a public library setting. The reason, without wishing to over-simplify, is because that user group is transient and highly flexible in its approach to learning. Typically the learning is boundless in time and scope, it is highly constructive and it can be subjective and personal.

Having said this, those library users who wish to use the library for informal learning pursuits, such as our Chesterfield library user quoted earlier, will often hone their information literacy skills through regular contact with library staff; although there is only anecdotal evidence to back this up, it does seem quite plausible.

When we talk about the role of libraries in supporting learners, this support is achieved primarily through the exploitation of the resources held in libraries; the books, journals, electronic sources etc. and also through the skills that trained library staff can offer. These skills entail analysing the information need, retrieving, evaluating and the presenting of information by the library worker on behalf of the learner. The whole relationship between library worker and user is often seen as a teacher–learner relationship. Yet this is always dependent, to a lesser or greater extent, on the resources and facilities held within the bounds of the library.[4]

Increasingly, from the library management perspective, the nature of the support from library staff poses a challenge. This challenge appears to be universal; while it may, in public libraries, follow a model different from that used in other libraries for example higher education libraries, the fundamental underpinning question is the same. What are the skills needed by staff to support learners? To understand the nature of this challenge one needs to look at how learning has evolved in recent times.

The more enlightened recognised the opportunity offered by the general shift in the traditional educational paradigm brought about by technology. Learning is no longer a simple exchange of information from the teacher to the learner. A more complex set of processes are undergone in order to provide a richer learning experience. Many within public libraries recognise the need to build upon the indirect approach of passively supporting instructivist learning and moving towards an engagement with the constructivist learner (Hein, 1991).[5]

The new learning paradigm sees learners learning through the act of information seeking rather than information finding. This is now somewhat at odds with those library workers who see their role simply as providing information for the learner. The library workers' role expands from provider of materials to one where facilitating discussion and developing collaborative learning become everyday tasks.

Here, we can be reminded of the monocultural approach to cooking that existed 40 years ago. The single-minded simplicity of 'meat and two veg' was accepted as efficient and, to be frank, was seen as the only option. The globalisation of the food industry, foreign travel and more ethnically diverse populations has revolutionised eating habits, and has educated, beyond expectation, the palette of the native population. While the tourist may approach the Sushi bar with considerably more trepidation than the learner approaches the library counter, the belief and willingness to experience something novel is common to both.

We should understand that public libraries in their early years have been a significant source of support for all types of learners since the Mechanics Institute movement of the mid-nineteenth century. The strength of the library then had been to passively provide support without seeking to shape or influence the direction of the learner. Subsequent to this early role for libraries there emerged a greater reliance on a systemic approach that saw the librarian control more resources as the technology to do so evolved. The librarian was placed as the intermediary between the enquirer/learner and the resources (Lock and Norden, 2000).

This era may be seen also (in learning terms) as spawning the standardised training programme. This enabled training providers through technology to administer many students and to avail of economies of scale. A narrowing and shallowing of learning generally gave rise, for example in schools, to the national curriculum. Lifelong learning will always suffer from being lead by two uncomfortable bedfellows: the 'learn to earn' ideal versus the personal self-fulfillment ideal (Edwards, 1999). The former, supported at every opportunity by policy makers has gained the ascendancy and has exploited the benefits inherent in the new media technologies, not for the betterment of the learner, but instead to gain economic advantage. The first wave of e-learning simply accelerated the final stage in the commodification of instruction-based teaching. Formal learning, delivered through established institutions (and by extension their libraries) standardised learning and the approaches to its support. In public libraries meanwhile, it is informal learning that flourishes and the individual who benefits. Informal learning appears unquantifiable, uncontrolled, even chaotic, but it remains the life-blood of the public library movement.

As we return again to our dinner table, it may be useful to contemplate how we choose our food – we may be reminded of the slight but ever-significant movement away from a battery farm approach to providing eggs towards the more enlightened free-range organic approach.

Dessert: supporting digital citizenship

The third course, the dessert course, should allow the main course to be digested. Here, we are looking at information literacy enabling, supporting and sustaining digital citizenship. In general terms there has been a rush to develop computer technology skills within the public library workforce. This was undertaken in response to the increasing demand from the public for access to information that was only accessible via the Internet. In public libraries the infrastructure was built with the financial support of the New Opportunities Funding (NOF). The resultant network of computers placed in public libraries with Internet connections was named the People's Network. This huge leap forward saw the introduction of new technology into public libraries coupled with a funded training programme:

> The People's Network project has three main strands: £100 million for the network infrastructure as part of the New Opportunities Fund Community Access to Lifelong Learning (People's Network) programme, £20 million to train all 40,000 library workers to use and help members of the public to use this equipment, and the opportunity to take part in the £50 million NOF-digitise content creation programme. The project has been running for just over a year now, and significant progress has been made in each key area. (Baigent, 2000)

Many within the library profession see the People's Network as a landmark, a major success in a landscape littered with the failed ICT projects of so many other professions. Certainly, this large mobilisation has been successful in terms of its own project – that is, it has stayed within budget and generally has been delivered within the targeted timescale. However, taking a step back there are certain issues that are still outstanding regarding the uses of ICT in public libraries. Library managers were quick to see the modernising effects the new technology would have, not to mention the sexiness and indeed the high impact of the new computer set against the backdrop of fading book covers. Yet there does not seem to be any evidence of wholesale commitment from local authorities to an overall strategic view of how the new ICT might be exploited to develop the public library movement.

The benefits and spin-offs were identified early on, but as for a clear overarching plan, none seems to have existed or, if a vision did exist, it was not shared effectively. Rather, there was a speedy introduction of the hardware that left large groups of staff at best confused and at worst feeling threatened. The delivery of formal training amounted to key-pressing routines and had little, if any, theoretical grounding, let alone any contextual explanation of why ICT was needed. This situation left a group of staff 'qualified' to a particular level in ICT skills serving a user base that, in general, could be regarded as being already inherently skilled in ICT and so requiring less and less assistance from the trained library staff. The overriding and default assumption was that the customer base pre-People's Network would continue to be the dominant customer base post-People's Network. This has not been the case. New, Internet savvy users have used the library ICT facilities. As the first wave of computer empowerment washed over the library user, library staff more often than not struggled with long queues and printers with paper jams.

So, although there has been a mass education of library workers and a general up-skilling, it seems that the linkages between this workforce development and a more direct strategic deployment of ICT have not been clearly made. It is of course easy to identify such shortcomings with the benefit of hindsight. In general those within the public library movement who, in the fading days of the twentieth century fought hard to ensure public libraries seized the opportunity, should not be forgotten nor should their achievement be underestimated. They built the infrastructure upon which tomorrow's public library will flourish. The up-skilling that went in tandem has provided library workers with the means to use technology and, if those skills can be developed further as part of an information literacy programme, much will have been achieved.[6]

The pace of technological change is unrelenting. A decade ago saw the dichotomy outlined above: we struggled constantly to separate the skills that are associated with ICT from those of the information-literate citizen. Today this struggle is perhaps no longer needed. So much of the information required today is available digitally and more to the point so much of the technology today is in fact seamless. What is really required is the ability to filter, evaluate and manage the actual content. Witness the use of MP3 players – though this nanotechnology is more or less invisible, the real challenges for the user are twofold. The first is overcoming the human–computer interface, in other words how to understand the different menu options or how to navigate the system. The second challenge is more closely related to what might be an accepted view of IL in that it is the task of generating, evaluating and organising content; in this case, that content is the music on an MP3 player.

The advent, in recent years, of electronic service delivery within public libraries has been similar to the acceptance into the domestic home of the microwave oven. Distrusted from its inception by many, and still to this day villified by traditionalists, the microwave, and perhaps more precisely its method of cooking, has had to fight hard for credibility. Today it is accepted as a labour-saving device upon which cooks are, to a large extent, dependent. The microwave oven is a tool in the same way that electronic service delivery can be seen as a tool.

Citizenship is a complex concept, digital citizenship even more so. Mostly it is a combination of the rights and responsibilities held by each member of society. The digital aspect implies that there is some electronic communication associated with the act of being an engaged citizen. These acts could range from participating via a local authority's online poll in a debate about local land use issues to the act of voting in a full-blown e-democracy.

When assessing the suitability of the public library to support digital citizenship the important point to note is that the People's Network provides the first prerequisite; the hardware infrastructure and telecommunications connectivity. The second prerequisite is the content, the information and the applications. The level of preparedness for this second step is quite low. Much of the engagement of the citizen that was expected by government is simply not there. Entertainment content delivered via the web is more popular and heavily used than the more serious information content. So, the policy document Framework for the Future places emphasis on digital citizenship yet provides little guidance on how to move towards its realisation. There can however be little doubt that at some stage the principles of information literacy will need to be deployed in the process of shaping a digital citizen. Moreover, a digital citizen will, by necessity, be information literate.

Cigars and brandy

During the Autumn of 2006 a group of staff, part of Bradford Council's public library service, undertook a unique and innovative learning programme. The subject that was being studied was information literacy and the method used to deliver the learning content was a virtual learning environment (VLE) called Moodle.[7] The course was named Pop-i and had been derived from an information literacy learning programme developed by Imperial College London. The cohort of 14 learners, taken from frontline and supervisory levels, were supported by two tutors who worked for Bradford's libraries. All were new to the concept of information literacy and its possible uses within a public library setting. The course comprised 10 learning units covering a theoretical introduction with definitions of IL followed by a range of practical explanations of key concepts, terms and applications that culminated in a module on future technologies and Web 2.0 deployments. A final and crucial module was the toolkit; the purpose of which was to pull together the knowledge and skills gained and to place them in a format that enabled the staff to transfer those skills to the end user in the library. Each module had, on completion, an assessment exercise this gave the learner the opportunity to assess how well they had done in terms of understanding and retaining the knowledge they had gained. There was a half-day face-to-face introduction to the course and at the close a focus group was held in order to gain feedback from learners and tutors. While this focus group gave good qualitative data, the use of reflective journals by the learners themselves provided rich, personal and often honest feedback. Quantitative data such as amount of time spent in the VLE was also gathered.

The findings point to several interesting issues. For example, all learners thought that there was a clear need for IL within public libraries with many expressing the sentiment that they were in fact, albeit in an ad-hoc way, already adhering to many of the IL principles and practices. The use of e-learning and in particular the high level of support was much appreciated. The library is now exploring other potential uses for its VLE, and hopes to harness the current enthusiasm and to develop further content.

Concluding on this positive note, it is quite probable that information literacy will within the coming years gain a foothold within public libraries. As demonstrated from the Pop-i project in Bradford there would appear to be support for a framework that enables staff to utilise their skills to assist users with general enquiries, informal and formal lifelong learning and with the emerging digital citizenship agenda.

Notes

1. For a general sociological background to the allotments movement, see Bourke (1994) and 'Allotments for the poor' (1882); p. 510.
2. A full treatment of the origins of the Public Library movement from various perspectives, such as working-class consciousness, social control and technical education, is provided in Black (1996). For a detailed outline of the general developments of the public library movement, see also Kelly (1973).
3. For an interesting perspective on the European dimension, see Coffield (1999).
4. As the lifelong learning agenda emerged in public libraries, so too did a role for librarians. A good example of one type of learning support activity undertaken is contained in Allred (2000). See also the original research (Allred and Allred, 1999).
5. For a philosophical (rather than learning theory) account of constructivism and associated meta-theories in relation to information science, see Talja, Tuominen, and Savolainen (2005; pp. 79–101).
6. For an early discussion of the impact of the web and the perceived change in the role on the librarian, see Wilson (1995). For an assessment of the key change drivers and impacts on the library and information services sector, see isNTO (2003). Also see Van Brakel, quoted in Raitt (1997).
7. 'Moodle is a course management system (CMS) – a free, Open Source

software package designed using sound pedagogical principles, to help educators create effective online learning communities. You can download and use it on any computer you have handy (including webhosts), yet it can scale from a single-teacher site to a 50,000-student University.' Moodle Homepage (2007); available at *http://www.moodle.org* (accessed January 2007).

References

Allred, J. (2000) 'The origins, activities and outcomes of the UK Department for Education and Employment's "Open for Learning" project 1992–1995', in *The New Review of Libraries and Lifelong Learning*, vol. 1. Cambridge: Taylor-Graham; pp. 103 –22.

Allred, J. and Allred, J. (1999) *Open Learning in Public Libraries: Impact on End Users*, research report 101. London: Department for Education and Employment.

Anonymous (1882) 'Allotments for the poor', *The Gardeners' Magazine*, September 23: 510.

Baigent, H. (2000) 'The people's network', *D-Lib Magazine*, 6(11): available at *http://www.dlib.org/dlib/november00/11inbrief.html#BAIGENT* (acessed January 2007).

Black, A. (1996) *A New History of The English Public Library – Social and Intellectual Contexts, 1850–1914*. Leicester: Leicester University Press.

Bourke, J. (1994) *Working-Class Cultures in Britain 1890–1960*. London: Routledge.

Coffield, F. (1999) *Why is the Beer Always Stronger Up North? Studies of Lifelong Learning in Europe*. Bristol: The Policy Press.

Coffield, F. (2000) 'The structure below the surface: reassessing the significance of informal learning', in F. Coffield (ed) *The Necessity of Informal Learning*. Bristol: The Policy Press; pp. 1 –11.

Comedia (1993) *Borrowed Time? The Future of Public Libraries in the UK*. Bourne Green: Comedia.

Delors, J. (1996) *Learning: The Treasure Within*. Paris: UNESCO.

Department of Culture, Media and Sport (2003) *Framework for the Future – Libraries Learning and Information in the Next Decade*. London: DCMS.

Eco, U. (1983) *The Name of the Rose* (W. Weaver, translator). New York: Warner.

Kelly, T. (1973) *A History of Public Libraries in Great Britain. 1845–1965*. London: The Library Association.

Edwards, R. (1999) *Changing Places? Flexibility Lifelong Learning and a Learning Society*. New York: Routledge.

Fritch, J.W. and Mandernack, S.B. (2001) 'The emerging reference paradigm: a vision of reference services in a complex information environment', *Library Trends*, 50(2): 286–305.

Hein, G. (1991) 'Constructivist learning theory, the museums and the needs of people', presentation at CECA (International Committee of Museum Educators) conference; available at *http://www.exploratorium.edu/IFI/resources/constructivistlearning.html* (accessed January 2007).

isNTO (Information Services National Training Organisation) (2003) *Skills Foresight in the Information Services Sector 2003–2009.* London: isNTO.

Lock, D. and Norden, J. (2000) 'Hybrid librarians and distance learners: the fact controllers?', in *The New Review of Libraries and Lifelong Learning*, vol. 1. Cambridge: Taylor Graham; pp. 137–54.

Proctor, R. and Bartle, C. (2002) *Low Achievers, Lifelong Learners. An Investigation into the Impact of the Public Library on Educational Disadvantage.* The University of Sheffield Library and Information Commission Research Report no. 117. Sheffield: Dept. of Information Studies, Centre for the Public Library and Information in Society.

Razzell, P.E. and Wainwright, R.W. (eds) (1973) *The Victorian Working Class – Selections from Letters to the Morning Chronicle* (letters first published 1849–51). London: Frank Cass & Company Limited; p. 55.

Talja, S, Tuominen, K. and Savolainen, R. (2005) '"Isms" in information science: constructivism, collectivism and constructionism', *Journal of Documentation*, 61(1): pp. 79–101.

Van Brakel, P. (1997) 'Education and training for information professionals in face of the Internet and World Wide Web', in D. Raitt (ed) *Libraries for the New Millennium – Implications for Managers.* London: Library Association Publishing; pp. 240–82

Wilson, J. (1995) 'Enter the cyberpunk librarian: future directions in cyberspace', *Library Review*, 44(8): 63–72.

3

Healthy mind, healthy body: digital literacy in the NHS

Di Millen and Helen Roberts

So, what's a chapter about digital literacy doing in a book about information literacy (IL)? Isn't that a bit like including a recipe about how to boil an egg in a 'gastro' cookbook?

In a world where IT is becoming as important as pen and paper as a means of managing and communicating information, as important as culinary staples like salt and sugar are to cooking, having the basic skills required to use the technology safely and effectively is a core skill. In culinary analogy terms, it's a little like investing in a fabulous, top of the line 'range' cooker and not knowing how to use it to best effect. At best, you end up with a burnt cake or raw meat. At worst, you revert to 'old' technology or takeaways!

'Information literacy' and 'digital literacy' are terms sometimes used synonymously. Whilst inextricably linked, they are in fact very different things. Digital literacy might be considered the foundation for information literacy – a prerequisite, essential for the effective use of the technology that is key to the management of data and information.

Given the availability of personal computers (PCs) in public libraries, schools and workplaces, as well as millions of homes in the UK, one might expect the basic IT skills gap to be so small as to not concern us here. There are, however, large numbers of the population that do not have, or will not acknowledge the requirement for, essential IT skills. This is particularly the case for those of middle age who did not have access to computers at school, or do not have children who expect to be able to create their own blogs and 'Google' for content for school projects and home work.

Being able to use a PC is now a skill for all and a skill for life, not just work. Being PC literate (digitally literate) is now as important, it is claimed, as being able to read and write.

Essential IT Skills in the NHS

The NHS in England[1] is modernising the delivery of patient care to improve service, outcomes and experiences. NHS Connecting for Health (NHS, 2007a) is an Agency of the Department of Health charged with delivery the National Programme for IT (NPfIT). Technology is being used to:

- enable patients to book their own outpatient appointments;
- provide electronic summary patient records, giving access to authorised personnel to critical information about medication and pre-existing conditions wherever and whenever the patient requires treatment;
- digitise x-ray and scan results, allowing rapid access, remote diagnosis and manipulation, and reducing storage requirements and reliance on toxic chemicals;
- support the electronic transfer of records between general practitioners (GPs) when a patient moves house/area;
- digitise the issue and management of prescriptions and associated payment processes.

The above is an indicative list only, included to demonstrate the growing importance of technology in clinical care and practice. Clinicians are increasingly expected to contribute to, and rely upon, evidence-based care in their routine practice. As Director of the National Knowledge Service, Professor Sir Muir Gray has said 'Knowledge is the enemy of disease' (NHS, 2007b). And clinicians increasingly have to accept the availability of clinical information on the Internet, and the fact that patients may often think they have more information than the specialist they have come to consult!

The NHS is purportedly the largest employer in Europe, with a workforce of around 1.3 million. It is estimated that at least 800,000 staff will need to use one or more of the new systems and technologies being introduced. They will only be able to do this if they have the skills and confidence to use a PC, even if only at a basic level. Indeed, some suppliers of the new systems (Local Service Providers) charged with delivering systems training have required the demonstration of basic skills as a prerequisite.

Therefore, if any NHS employee is going to be trained in a new system, or use data and information effectively for research to support improvements in patient care, they must have the basics in place. Whilst at present it may be possible for healthcare professionals – clinicians and others – to avoid using IT, in the not too distant future there will be no escape and no acceptable excuses for not knowing how to start.

Many clinical and professional educational programmes (under- and postgraduate, pre- and post-registration) now include a requirement to use office-type applications (word processing and spreadsheet software) for assignments and projects. Basic or essential skills are, however, rarely taught, and even more rarely based on an agreed standard, and then assessed.

Whilst most, if not all, NHS organisations now have or have access to a computer-based training centre, there is never enough capacity to meet all the local organisations' needs. As the NPfIT systems are deployed, essential IT skills training competes with other ongoing and systems training. NHS librarians can provide an additional and important resource. Not only do they have the necessary skills themselves, but they see the application of these skills in clinical information contexts on a daily basis.

Much of the training currently offered in the NHS is of a self-taught nature, using either intranet or web-based resources. The focus of this chapter is therefore on the role of the librarian or other professional in the delivery of face-to-face training for NHS staff and in particular members of clinical professions.

Too many cooks?

There are many examples of good, effective collaboration between health librarians and their local information, IT and IM&T training departments, for example around:

- supporting training for clinicians in 'The Map of Medicine' (Informa Healthcare, 2007);
- supporting training in local electronic document management systems and intranets;
- negotiating with public libraries colleagues around use of their public PCs for outpatient appointment booking.

Indeed, the cross-referral of trainees between hospital IT departments and NHS libraries can be used to support applications for health library accreditation (NHS, 2005a). As in a busy but efficient modern restaurant kitchen, objectives are best achieved when supported by clear, shared objectives, with good team work, excellent communication and clear lines of responsibility and accountability. Therefore, a dialogue and collaboration between the health librarian and the local IT or IM&T training manager are crucial elements of the successful recipe.

Preparation, phase 1

Before embarking on any IT skills training or support, the following checklist might help (talk to the local IT or IM&T training manager too, but before you do, try some personal research to establish the following points):

1. What is the local strategy and plan for developing basic (essential) IT skills? For example, is it based on the national reference standard, the European Computer Driving Licence (ECDL)3 or some other alternative?

2. Is there a local training centre, and if so, when is it open (office hours only or evenings/nights) and what does it offer?

3. How many trainers are there?

4. How many clinicians use the training facility?

5. At what stage is the organisation at in its deployment of new systems, and what are its priorities?

6. What is the balance between self-teaching and classroom-based learning approaches within the organisation?

7. Are there any gaps or challenges where you might be able to help?

8. What local training resources are used, and how might you complement these?

Health librarians can often provide added value in the shape of case studies and appropriately contextualised examples and content that make the basic skills training more relevant, and, therefore, more interesting, to clinicians.

Top Tip

Basic web searching skills might be taught by asking delegates to open up a web browser and search for an accredited clinical information repository via the National Library for Health (NHS, 2005b); or by searching Medline (NHS, 2005c) or the Cochrane Library (Wiley, 2007).

Preparation, phase 2: drafting the menu

So, once you know what the required ingredients are, and what your role in the kitchen is going to be, what else might you need to consider when drafting your menu?

Your target audience

Consider the nature of your target audience. Most health libraries are associated with local postgraduate medical education and health studies departments, and as such are ideally – but not exclusively – suited to offering clinically-orientated courses and support.

Keep the pace of the delivery snappy and challenging. Don't let your audience get bored, but remember that some delegates might find it hard to admit they are struggling or don't understand – particularly if your session includes a mix of specialities, professions and/or grades. Getting the content right is also crucial. Undertaking a training needs assessment in advance of the course will help identify those who will need more in the way of time and support than others and provide a guide to the level and pace you will need to apply. ECDL 'Getting Started' (see below) is certainly worth looking at in this context.

Use of language

Think about your use of language. We have used the terms 'basic IT skills', 'essential IT skills' and 'literacy' throughout this chapter. NHS Connecting for Health has deliberately changed the way it describes its ECDL service, from 'basic' to 'essential' IT skills, as a response to feedback that 'basic' was not an attractive description for many professionals in the Service. This is important in any marketing and promotional material, as well as during any training. Handle the use of language with tact!

Cherries or carrots?

Might some form of accreditation act as a 'cherry on the cake' or a 'carrot' to attract those for whom this is a key driver? If your local strategy includes encouraging staff to work towards modules of the ECDL, this may be carrot enough, as research shows that the qualification is attractive to the whole range of health service professionals. Recognition by professional bodies, however, might be a further incentive, as might a certificate of attendance or similar for use in continuous professional development portfolios.

As an incentive for individuals to embark on a skills programme and to get them interested in the technology in the first place, some health organisations have made PCs available at different times and at different locations (such as in the staff dining room) loaded with non-work-related software such as language skills programmes and other self-teaching packages. Local policies on this approach vary and some are worried that making such facilities available will result in staff being distracted from their important role in patient care and support. Arguments can be made either way, so local views and the culture of the organisation will need to be considered.

Top Tip

Confidence comes with familiarity. Consider making a PC available for social and personal use by staff (checking out the local PC security rules and firewall issues first) and assess the appropriateness of encouraging students to practice their mouse skills by playing 'solitaire' as part of their essential skills course. Use Amazon (*http://www.amazon.co.uk*), eBay (*http://www.ebay.co.uk*) and lastminute.com (*http://www.lastminute.com*) as well as *http://www.informatics.nhs.uk* and *http://www.library.nhs.uk* as sites worthy of a visit as part of your course.

Network and connectivity issues

Be clear about local strategies and issues relating to links between the NHS secure private network 'N3' and the academic network, 'Janet'. In some organisations, their technical solutions will have been put into place to enable professionals based at teaching hospitals (universities) to access, seamlessly, the entire NHS network. In others, the two systems may not talk to each other and this can be a real irritation to users. As a trainer, it may restrict your ability to access data and websites, so be prepared and plan your sessions accordingly.

Location, location, location

Health libraries are often restricted in the amount of space and number of PCs available for training. It may be possible to use other local rooms and kit, but there may be a need to offer one-to-one or one-to-two sessions rather than group courses. This will affect your style, timetable and the degree of interactivity you need to plan for.

Tactically, offering one-to-one training and coaching in the postgraduate library might prove attractive to clinicians, although time-consuming for you! The library might well be seen as a safe and familiar haven and therefore attract individuals who would otherwise slip through the net. Programmes of skills training should be planned accordingly.

Ingredients

The ECDL qualification is available to all NHS staff in England, Wales and Northern Ireland through a scheme managed centrally by NHS Connecting for Health. 'Getting started' is designed especially to help new PC users to get going, with the support of a trainer as a pre-ECDL option, supported by an online skills assessment tool. There are more than 120,000 registered learners and over 350 learning and test centres. The ECDL qualification is available at three levels:

- British Computer Society Level 1: passing all 1, 2 and 7 modules.
- ECDL: passing all 7 modules (not all at once!).
- British Computer Society Level 2: modules 3, 4, 5 and 6 of the ECDL plus module E.

The seven modules are:

1. Basic Concepts of IT
2. Using the Computer and Managing Files
3. Word Processing
4. Spreadsheets
5. Databases
6. Presentations
7. Information and Communication

In addition, a module specifically for health and care staff is also available covering aspects associated with the special nature of data and information in health, particularly those around security and confidentiality. More information is available at *http://www.ecdl.nhs.uk*.

Top Tip

> Don't try to reinvent the wheel. Check out *http://www.ecdl.nhs.uk* for information about what ECDL is, and access the online trainers' toolkit. Register as a member of the ETD (education, training and development) Special Interest Group (SIG) on *http://www.informatics.nhs.uk* to access people, information and resources. Local trainers generally have a network group – virtual and physical – to tap into, and the SIG is a good place to start.
>
> Consider taking the qualification yourself as the best way of getting to know its content and level and to know best how to prepare others for take the tests.

There are several alternatives to the ECDL, such as the Information Technology Qualification (ITQ), CLAIT and CLAIT Plus, and a 'Digital Literacy' qualification offered by Microsoft. The NHS will continue to support ECDL as the national reference standard at least until spring 2008, with the associated scheme providing centrally purchased log books, training materials and tests.

Timing

Many clinical professionals work long shifts and out of normal office hours. Offering training in the evenings and at the end of shifts may be an option worth considering. As part of the overall blend, consideration could be given to the use of CD or web-based training materials that individuals can use at a time, place and pace to suit them. The local trainer might then provide remote support and advice and or the opportunity for supplementary coaching on a one-to-one basis when time and shift patterns allow.

The faculty

Experience has shown that clinicians relate well to peers in learning and development situations, particularly in group sessions. Is there a local knowledgeable and skilled clinician who has excellent communication skills and levels of enthusiasm to tap into?

Are there others in the organisation or local health community who might be willing and able to help develop and deliver courses tailored to the needs and expectations of your target audience?

The main course

The nature of your audience, their backgrounds and professional groupings, degrees of familiarity with technology and a range of other issues will influence your style, content and its contextualisation and delivery. One recipe will not suit everyone, so be prepared to add some extra seasoning, remove optional ingredients and replace sweet with sour, if necessary!

The following are pointers to key issues to consider when putting your offer together:

- Getting the pitch, tone and level of your presentation right is often a challenge. The one thing to avoid at all costs is patronising people.

- As we have already said, consider the pace. Plan to keep it snappy, but be prepared to adapt as required.

- Skills are best taught, and behaviour most likely to be changed, by seeing and doing, not listening. Even background and understanding can be taught in a practical way by actively engaging of your students.

> Learning is the process of active engagement with experience. It is what people do when they want to make sense of the world. It may involve the development or deepening of skills, knowledge, understanding, awareness, values, ideas and feelings, or an increase in the capacity to reflect. Effective learning leads to change, development and the desire to learn more. (Museums, Libraries and Archives Council, 2004. Quoted in Webb and Powis, 2004)

Clinicians are, by nature, scientists. Although this is a gross generalisation, think about taking an appropriate approach to delivery.

Decide whether a formal or informal (or mix of the two) style is most appropriate for your audience.

Top Tip

Essential skills courses often include an introduction to the nature of hardware and software. ECDL Module 1, for example, is called 'Basic Concepts of IT'. It covers some of the basic concepts of information technology such as data storage and memory, the context for computer-based software applications in society, and the uses of information networks within computing.

Consider including a PC 'dissection' in your session. Your students could gather around a 'dissecting' table and observe the dismantling of the hardware. Pass round the hard drive and other parts and then allow a small group to put it all back together again.

Getting started with ECDL

First impressions are so important in many aspects of personal and business life. Making the right impression and getting the basics right with new students may determine both how much they learn and how much they want to learn more.

Top Tip

To capture your students' imaginations, and amaze them with the power of the Internet, log onto the web and, using a search engine of your choice, ask them to challenge you to find some information, e.g. what time does the National Portrait Gallery in London open on Saturday; or find a photograph of a small (named) hotel in Cuba (be prepared, however, for sites to be unavailable or for your Internet connection to go down – see below).

The following plans have been proven successful in getting groups of NHS clinicians started with their ECDL qualification when the expectation is that they will work through the materials on a self-taught basis, whether or not classroom-based or one-to-one training is to be provided.

ECDL Getting Started for Clinicians		
Date: 06/08/2006	Name of tutor:	H. Roberts
Location: Room No:	Training Suite, Hospital Site 1	Number of learners: 6 Duration of session: 2 hrs
Prerequisites:	• Preferable to have basic keyboard and mouse skills • Should have an e-mail account • Should have completed an ECDL Learning Agreement • Should have completed a TNA before commencement of the ECDL course	
Aim of session: *To enrol Clinicia(s) onto the NHS ECDL portal to enable access to their learning via the NHS ECDL portal and be able to use the portal for study.*		
Objectives: *To register individual(s) onto the NHS European Computer Driving Licence (ECDL) Project.*		
Resources required: 6 PCs with Internet access Wipe board, pens and eraser	Handouts: • ECDL booklet • Registration form • Learning contract • Matrix forms for training needs analysis (Modules 2 and 7) • Self-registration help instructions • Download instructions	Room layout:
Session outline		
Timing	Element	Additional notes:
10 mins	Introduction	
5 mins	Aims and objectives	
1hr 10 mins	Session content	
25 mins	Recap and questions	
10 mins	Next steps	

ECDL Getting Started for Clinicians: lesson plan

Aim of session

To enrol Clinician(s) onto the NHS ECDL portal to enable access to their learning via the NHS ECDL portal and be able to use the portal for study.

Objectives

- To register individual(s) onto the NHS European Computer Driving Licence (ECDL) project
- To introduce and familiarise the learner with the NHS ECDL training portal
- To have completed a self-assessment on ECDL Modules 2 and 7
- To agree timescales and training plan

Duration of session

2 hrs

Equipment/materials required

- PC with Internet access
- Handouts (examples below)
- Evaluation sheet to be handed out at end of the session for any learners to complete

Handouts

- ECDL booklet
- Registration form
- Learning contract
- Matrix forms for training needs analysis (Modules 2 and 7)
- Self-registration help sheet
- Download instructions

Prerequisites

- Preferable to have basic keyboard and mouse skills
- Should have an e-mail account
- Should have completed an ECDL learning agreement
- Should have completed a TNA before commencement of the ECDL course

Introduction

Welcome and introduction by trainer
Directions to toilets and fire escape
Health and safety, i.e. chair height, lighting, etc.
Outline of session and objectives
Questions answered throughout session

Outline of session

1. Introduction

- ECDL overview
- How ECDL works – the modules explained
- The benefits to the individual and working environment
- Training and support available

2. Paperwork and assessment

- Fill in paperwork
- Completion of any self-assessment

3. NHS ECDL logbook voucher

- Completion of the NHS ECDL logbook voucher

4. Self-registration

- Registration onto the NHS ECDL project via the training portal

5. Training resources

- Explanation of and familiarisation with the training materials available on the NHS portal
- Scheduled training sessions and workshops available

6. Training plan

- To agree timescales and plan training with designated ECDL trainer

Recap of session

- Review objectives to ensure these have been met
- Evaluation sheet to be handed out at end of the session for any learner(s) to complete

Dealing with disasters: coping with burnt toast

If one thing is certain, the technology itself will represent one of the greatest challenges you will face in delivery a successful course – whether it be basic IT skills or a more advanced information retrieval course further along the information literacy continuum.

Therefore, be prepared:

- Expect the technology to fall over, as forewarned is forearmed. Have overhead projector slides ready as a back up resource, and take screenshots of the software and include them in your 'old technology' presentation just in case. Even this may not provide full protection. Overhead projectors only work when you have power, so the third fallback is to have printed copies of your presentation to hand so that students can at least have a reference copy in front of them (to take away as well). (The author commends this from her heart – a very difficult afternoon was once spent delivering a workshop during a power cut with no paper copies of slides to refer to and a dead battery in the laptop!)
- Live Internet-based demonstrations can be very powerful, as we have said, but be prepared for links to be dead and connections to drop, and for sites to be unavailable.

Coffee and mints

The evaluation of training is difficult and something that is often paid only lip service to. 'Happy sheets' may tell you a little, but not enough, and assessing the longer-term impact of essential skills training is problematic to say the least.

The business justification for investment in any training, including essential IT skills training, and the perceived benefits to the organisation are likely to determine levels of executive support and consequent resource allocations. So, difficult or not, those managing and delivering skills training will be required to evaluate activity and demonstrate value for money.

Top Tips

- Design a training questionnaire that you can use for both pre- and post-course analysis, perhaps based on the syllabus for 'Getting Started'. This will at least give you a basic quantitative indication of the skill and confidence levels of students after their experience.

- Check out the NHS ECDL website for tools and links to tools that might be helpful (*http://www.ecdl.nhs.uk*) and talk to other local trainers who may have existing resources you could use or adapt.

- Ask users about how often they need to ask for assistance, and ask them to describe their levels of confidence when using systems.

Other more qualitative measures you might want to consider are:

- Levels and nature of help desk calls – is there a demonstrable link between the delivery of essential IT skills training and either a drop in the number of help desk calls in general or a reduction in calls specifically associated with basic problems like minimising Windows or file management?

- Is the local IT department able to identify increases in the volume of e-mails, use of the intranet, or perhaps the National Electronic Library for Health following a programme of essential skills training?

- Has the demand for more advanced Office application training increased since the introduction of essential skills training – a possible indicator of increasing use of and confidence with software and hardware?

In addition, you may wish to:

- Revisit the qualitative questions from the pre-course analysis to assess changes in attitude and confidence.

- Consider undertaking a cost benefit analysis. The national Essential IT Skills service delivered by NHS Connecting for Health has published the results of a survey of ECDL 'graduates' in 2004–2005 (NHS, 2007c).Using a formula designed to calculate the impact of the service on nurses, the conclusion indicates that across all disciplines within the NHS the hours saved over a year exceeded the hours spent in learning, and the average time saved by nurses as a result of using the IT systems more efficiently and effectively was 29 minutes each day.

Washing up

Over time, the need for essential or 'basic' IT skills training and support is predicted to decline, and not just because as we leave school and further or higher education we will have acquired the core skills required for life as a citizen in the information age. As technology itself matures, it inevitably becomes more intuitive and more user friendly. Mobile phones are a good example of this: although size is reduced and functionality increased, the basic functions and keystrokes remain if not the same, then similar. PCs and their software are much the same.

So, basic IT skills are like some of the basic cookery skills still taught in schools today – like boiling an egg, making a cup of tea, and knowing the difference between 'simmer' and 'steam'. Whilst some of the ingredients will need to be modified over time – for example, as the kind of IT we use in our hospitals and out in our community care environments starts to use different input devices (moving from keyboards to character and voice recognition, for example) – the basic concepts will be the same and support for new or returning users will be required.

Over time, we may well see the technology becoming completely ubiquitous and the teaching of users performed in an integral fashion, but basic skills will always be required, wherever and however taught, and these will still be core to the ever increasing importance of information literacy in an information-dependent society.

Note

1. Each home country in the UK (England, Scotland, Wales and Northern Ireland) has its own NHS policies and strategies. This chapter discusses digital literacy from an English perspective.

References

Informa Healthcare (2007) *Map of Medicine.* Available at *http://www. mapofmedicine.com/* (accessed 10 February 2007).

NHS (2005a) *National Electronic Library for Health Accreditation of Health Libraries.* Available at *http://www.nelh.nhs.uk/librarian/accreditation.asp* (accessed 10 February 2007).

NHS (2005b) *National Electronic Library for Health.* Available at *http://www.nelh.nhs.uk/* (accessed 10 February 2007).

NHS (2005c) *National Electronic Library for Health: Medline.* Available at *http://www.nelh.nhs.uk/medline/* (accessed 10 February 2007).

NHS (2007a) *Connecting for Health.* Available at *http://www. connectingforhealth.nhs.uk/* (accessed 10 February 2007).

NHS (2007b) *National Knowledge Service.* Available at *http://www.nks.nhs.uk/* (accessed 10 February 2007).

NHS (2007c) *Connecting for Health Marketing and Publications.* Available at *http://www.ecdl.nhs.uk/resources/marketingpublications* (accessed 10 February 2007).

Webb, J. and Powis, C. (2004) *Teaching Information Skills: Theory and Practice.* London: Facet Publishing.

The Cochrane Library (2007) Available at *http://www.thecochranelibrary.com* (accessed 10 February 2007).

4

Information discovery stir-fry: information literacy in the commercial sector

Angela Donnelly and Carey Craddock, Unilever R&D, UK

The commercial kitchen

In this chapter we will be exploring information literacy (IL) practices from within commercial organisations. Commercial libraries can be found across a variety of sectors including business, legal, manufacturing, pharmaceutical and fast moving consumer goods companies.

In 1998 these were more likely to be found in the pharmaceutical and chemical industries (SLA, 1998). In September 2006, total membership for the Chartered Institute of Library and Information Professionals (CILIP) stood at 21,388 and of this number around 7 per cent belonged to the Industrial and Commercial Libraries Special Interest Group. Specific details of which companies have corporate libraries can be found in numerous information sources, including British Library Directory of UK corporate libraries (British Library, 2003), Special Libraries Association (SLA) and CILIP. Most corporate libraries are funded as overheads and may be staffed by solo librarians or larger teams. They will all be required to provide a range of services, from inter-library loans to journal subscription management and provision of commercially-produced databases. They will almost certainly be involved in setting up and managing internal information sources and databases. Provision of some form of enquiry/current awareness service will also be a key function. Many small businesses may have no information function at all and will be reliant upon public libraries or Business Link services.

Commercial libraries have faced numerous challenges over the past decade. Companies have realised that good quality, timely and relevant information is to critical business processes and decisions (Reid, Thompson and Wallace-Smith, 2006). Consequently, this type of information is now more widely accessible to company employees due to the explosion of digital information and development of desktop retrieval systems (Abell, Skelton and Winterman, 2003). Much of this information is perceived to be 'free' on the Internet, so paradoxically, just at the time when staff are faced with increasing volumes of information to search through and manage, there is less demand for information from the corporate library and hence this core function has slowly diminished. As a result, libraries across the sector have faced downsizing and even closure (Kirton and Barham, 2005). Commercial organisations are also subject to constant change and reorganisation, not only internally but also on a larger scale resulting from any merger or takeover activity that may occur. This can also have an impact on the services provided.

Information professionals who have successfully evolved and survived these changes have done so because they have worked to understand both employee and business needs and have adapted accordingly (Scammell, 2001). It is from this process that information literacy training has emerged as new role for information professionals from within the commercial sector.

Commercial sector employees face enormous problems trying to handle information (O'Sullivan, 2002). It is considered to be a frustrating and time-consuming task. In a survey by Outsell Inc. in 2006 (Lustig 2006), it was found that searches performed by scientists on the Internet or an intranet were unsuccessful one third of the time.

In order to address this problem, the adoption of information literacy skills are essential, benefiting both the employees and the company. Bean (2001) includes the increasing rise in globalisation, routine need to access and utilise effectively increasingly sophisticated products including e-mail, the Internet and other desktop databases and the move away from the idea of having a 'job for life' as reasons why information literacy is now becoming more widespread in the commercial sector. This is also borne out by Lloyd (2003), who states that employees who are able to 'develop information pathways and to create new corporate knowledge provide the strategic difference between a highly successful business and those that remain mediocre'. Information literacy has also been reported to be one of the five essential competencies for solid job performance (Cheuk, 2002).

Evidence suggests that few companies have adequately addressed this issue. Knowledge management strategies have been implemented as a way of promoting the value of shared information (TFPL, 1999).

However, this has mainly resulted in the introduction of new technologies rather than basic information skills training (Kirton and Barham, 2005; O'Sullivan, 2002). This void has presented an ideal opportunity for information professionals in the commercial sector to demonstrate their value to the company. Taking ownership of an information literacy programme is even considered to be a 'survival tactic' by some corporate libraries (Wesson, 2006).

Information training by commercial librarians has now evolved from being 'point and click' on individual tools to taking on a more holistic approach. This could be in part due to the increasing number of end users entering the workplace from a university background who are already familiar with key sources and have had training on how to use them while in academia. Training is much about searching for and managing information as it is about ways of working.

Current practices

Information literacy is a relatively recent concept in commercial organisations. Its origins lie in American and Australian education theory and librarianship, and this is where much of the work has be completed and documented to date. It is widely recognised that information literacy training within the workplace is likely to be very different to IL programmes established in academic institutions (O'Sullivan, 2002). This is largely due to the fact that information is handled and managed very differently within the work environment (Kirton and Barham, 2005) and employees have different pressures and time constraints compared to students. Terminologies also differ; 'information literacy' is largely a label created and used by academic or public librarians and is not recognised in the business environment (O'Sullivan, 2002).

Most research into information literacy in the workplace is conceptual (Bruce, 1999). There are some case studies that provide evidence of IL training within businesses (Boelens, 2001; Donnelly and Craddock, 2002; Kirton and Barham, 2005; Wesson, 2006), but little evidence that this is becoming widespread in the commercial sector. Furthermore, practical guidance on how to develop an IL skills training within this sector is virtually non-existent (Cheuk, 2002).

Evidence suggest that it is usually the corporate library that has implemented the IL programmes, but sometimes other departments (such as Human Resources) manage this type of training (Wesson, 2006). A common theme/characteristic that emerges from all the case studies is that successful IL training within the commercial sector is adaptable, tailored and available at the point of need. Information professionals must be ready, willing and able to deliver training in whatever format is most appropriate at short notice to take advantage of requests for such help – the 'fast food' approach.

Ingredients/store cupboard

As in all good kitchens, a highly qualified team and a well-stocked store cupboard are essential to ensure smooth running.

Some of our basic essentials include:

- pre-cooked examples – 'ready meals' – that can be taken out and used at a moments notice;
- access to appropriate, quality information sources and databases;
- basic materials that you can use again and again, such as:
  - handouts;
  - tips sheets;
  - sample exercises and examples to cover a variety of topics;
  - diagrams;
  - web addresses;
  - registration forms for new users where passwords will be required;
- a range of materials to suit all learning types, such as websites (for those who prefer to learn alone), hands-on training, one to one training and demonstrations;
- a well qualified and enthusiastic 'head chef';
- suitable equipment, including:
  - access to computer(s);
  - data and/or overhead projector(s);
  - flipchart and pens;
- a suitable 'dining room' to deliver the training in.

Preparation

Training the cook – what do you need to know?

New practitioners will certainly benefit greatly from investing a good proportion of time familiarising themselves with the issues and practices surrounding the concept of 'information literacy'. This will enable you to provide a more inspiring menu, discover the recipes for success, and avoid cooking meals people simply do not want.

To a large extent, a general understanding of 'information literacy' can be sought from books, journals and websites. To maintain awareness of current issues that surround information literacy, you should also join discussion groups, attend annual conferences and network with fellow professionals who are involved in IL (see Further Information section below).

Attending relevant training sessions is also important if you either need to enhance your understanding of information literacy or to brush up on the essential skills needed to deliver an IL programme. There are various courses available that specifically focus on IL and a vast number relating to teaching, training and presentation skills. Consider attending IT-related courses that may help you develop the specific knowledge required for a basic training session (e.g. PowerPoint) or for creating a virtual learning environment (VLE)). You may also want to enhance your own information skills in order to feel confident about your subject knowledge. If so, there are plenty of courses available that cover IL related areas, including searching techniques and managing information (see Further Information section below).

The bigger picture...

It is certainly worthwhile to invest time and energy meeting workplace IL practitioners, who are usually more than happy to share their experiences with you. As already mentioned, some research has been carried out into companies who have developed IL programmes. To find more information it is worth searching out relevant bibliographic databases, for example LISA, ERIC or ABI Inform. Attending conferences such as LILAC is also an option, although these are usually attended by IL practitioners from the higher education sector and, while the principles remain the same, the customers and environment in which the commercial Library or Information Centre operates may be very different. Using online IL discussion forums such as LIS-INFOLITERACY can also be a very productive way of contacting other IL workplace practitioners. Joining CILIP groups such as *The Industrial and Commercial Libraries Group* would also be a good starting point.

Who's coming to the restaurant and what do they want?

Decisions need to made early on about which customers will require training and what it is they need. You would not, for example, offer beef bourguignon to a vegetarian, so knowing customer requirements in advance is important to avoid wasting time preparing training material that will simply never get used.

Think about your existing customers needs, and also about the people who have never used your services before but might be interested in IL training. Try not to make assumptions about the information skill levels of your customers or what they need. Talk to your customers, ask gently probing questions to tactfully ascertain their level of understanding and then pitch your training at their level. If you are alert then you will be able to find any evidence of training needs that may already be at your fingertips.

You may want to design your IL programme around specific 'groups' of customers who may have varying IL needs, e.g. new starters, project leaders, secretaries, research assistants. It may be more appropriate to produce sessions focussing on specific subject areas, e.g. information literacy for food science, toxicology or social sciences and so on. Alternatively, focus on specific topics that could be addressed by an IL training session, e.g. search skills for the Internet.

Your customer's food cravings – what you already know

A restaurateur will usually include on their menu some dishes frequently demanded by their customers on the basis that they are guaranteed 'winners'. Similarly, using the knowledge you already have about popular training issues can be used to help design your programme. Finding out about patterns in user behaviour can be useful (Bell, 2001). For example, checking the enquiries logged at the library help desk may reveal what type of training issues the customers are raising. Talk to colleagues who have direct contact with customers, such as help desk staff and information scientists, as they may also be knowledgeable about common customer training issues.

Top Tip

Aart van den Kuilen at Solvay Pharmaceuticals B.V. finds a number of his users have preferred sources that they go to time and time again without thinking about others that may be more appropriate. This is a common dilemma and can be resolved by including the old favourite in the training but comparing and contrasting to other sources so users can see the difference in the type of results they get.

But what about secret food cravings?

Identifying popular food dishes is usually easier than obtaining the full picture about peoples eating habits and food cravings. A restaurateur would be wise to find out this information and you should also approach customers to find out about in more detail what they want from an IL programme.

Try this informally by questioning customers at the help desk or during meetings. Organising a focus group is a more formal procedure and involves asking questions within an interactive group setting. It is advisable to invite a good cross-section of customers holding different positions from a variety of internal departments, and could potentially include non-users of the service (Bell, 2001; Oman, 2001). This may help you obtain very different perspectives of customer training needs. Focus group discussions can provide valuable feedback about the difficulties experienced in information handling and can help define the requirements for both content and format of the training programme.

Don't be too adventurous too soon – offer the favourites on the menu and experiment later

Once you have established the broad content of your IL programme, it is worth focussing initially on the development of just one aspect of this. Your customers may have told you they want a five-course meal, but in reality may only have the appetite or time to consume a snack.

Top Tip

At Unilever, three key areas were identified for the IL programme: *discovery*, *organisation* and *sharing* of information (Figure 4.1). These modules are all linked to the key stages in desktop research, i.e. finding literature, managing the data and dissemination of information (Orna and Stevens, 1995). Two initial modules were created: *Discovery* – focusing on information retrieval, searching techniques and source selection, and *Information Management* – including *organising* and *sharing* of information that we see as being complimentary to discovery.

A decision was made early on to focus efforts on the *discovery* element of the programme. There were very pragmatic reasons for this; for example it would:

- avoid wasting precious resources developing a complete training programme that is later only partially used;

- enable the trainers to test the water with the customers and find out if the content and format of the course met their needs;

- be popular and easy to sell, as it was evident the customers were very interested in information retrieval. Once interest in IL had been established other topics could then be introduced.

Figure 4.1   Information literacy themes

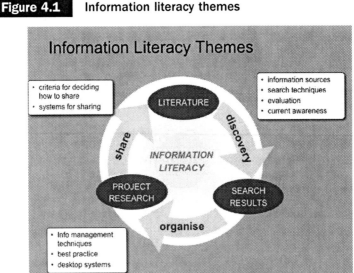

Once the broad content for your IL programme has been identified this needs to be broken down into a number of key areas. You can then start to consider how you will produce and deliver your training content. For example, an IL session that aims to help develop search strategies for electronic resources can be broken down in to a number of core elements:

- how to identify your main concepts and keywords;
- searching for word variations (use of truncation and wildcards);
- applying search operators (e.g. Boolean);
- use and application of parenthesis;
- refining your search (e.g. use of proximity operators, using limits).

Dividing up the core content in this way can allow you to mix and match different aspects of the course according to customer requirement and length of training session.

The kitchen team

A successful information literacy training programme cannot be achieved in isolation (Winkler, 2001). Working collaboratively with other information professionals within your organisation to develop an IL programme has enormous benefits (Scammell, 2001). Information literacy impacts on all areas of business, and a 'strategic approach is essential for commercial benefit' (Gasteen and O'Sullivan, 2000). Forming a good relationship with Human Resources (HR) can be highly productive. If there are standard competencies required of employees, it is worthwhile working with HR to integrate IL within skill profiles (Oman, 2001). HR may also be involved with training and development on a wider scale and may be able to help you get your IL programme on to the organisation's agenda. If other trainers operate within your organisation, they may also be able to provide valuable insights into your organisation's training culture (e.g. format preferences, length of session that is considered reasonable, or popular delivery methods).

Working productively with other internal information professionals can also be beneficial. For some courses it is important to have a level of subject specific knowledge (Thompson and Cronje, 2001). If you have colleagues with the in-depth subject specific knowledge required, enlist their help and support when planning your training sessions.

Top Tip

> Bring in a guest chef. Invite trainers provided by vendors of specialist tools to deliver training within organisations. These trainers are highly skilled and knowledgeable subject specialists, and will add a new dimension to the training already being delivered in-house. This has been undertaken at Unilever and leading pharmaceutical companies.

Preparing for each meal – what do you fancy from the menu?

In order to fully address your customers training needs you will need to investigate their current information practices. You could consider using a questionnaire for this purpose, but often a face-to-face discussion is more likely to give you the detail you require.

For example, if the IL training relates to information retrieval you should find out about problems encountered (e.g. finding too much information, don't know where to search etc.) and ask your customer how and where they currently search for information. Finding out about subject interests is also very important in order to tailor the IL sessions and produce relevant examples and exercises. Ask your customers to provide you with relevant documents (e.g. patents, journal articles or books) as this will enable you to understand their research area(s) in more depth. You can also pick out relevant keywords from these documents to produce example search strategies during the training session.

A brief plan of the training event is essential. This will help you focus on the structure of the training session and act as useful guide to you during delivery. This should include the timings of each section, detail of the content and delivery (practical exercise, demonstration etc.) and a reminder to you to provide handouts, additional information and so on.

Example session plan for using the Internet to carry out searches

Subject	Activity	Time
Introduction	Introduction Discussion of expected learning outcomes Practicalities – timings, format, using PCs	5 minutes
Self-assessment	Exercise Ask participants to carry out their own Internet search using a PC	10 minutes
Searching methods	*Slide* – facet breakdown *Demo* – in Google *Slide* – word variations *Slide* – searching for varied company names	10 minutes
Concepts and keywords	Exercise – use a concept grid to consider concepts and alternative keywords	5 minutes
Self-assessment	Exercise Ask participants to repeat their earlier search, this time using some of the new techniques covered in the session, and compare the results	10 minutes
Conclusion	Any questions? Brief summary of what has been covered Handout evaluation sheet	5 minutes

Prepare core content

As the recipe title suggests, taking the 'stir-fry' approach enables one to deliver the same core programme each time but with local variations to suit the tastes/needs of each group or individual. Preparation can be time-consuming, but once you have the basics ready, delivery can be quick and adaptations are relatively simple.

Method

Assess learning style and deliver so it appeals to all

In 1992, Honey and Mumford put forward the idea that people fall into four main groups with regard to learning style – activists, pragmatists, theorists and reflectors (Honey and Mumford, 1992). It is important when devising a programme to take all of these learning styles into account and to try to ensure there is something for all in each session. It is worth considering the possibility of a link between the learning style of an individual and their 'information style'. Sheila O'Flynn, now an independent information specialist, examined the possibility that an 'information activist', for example, might be more likely to network and try out new tools but would be less inclined to spend time planning a search strategy, while an 'information theorist' would do a thorough prior art search but would find it much harder to reach an end point. This has also since been demonstrated by others (Heinstrom, 2005; Donnelly and Craddock, 2002; Thompson and Cronje, 2001). If a team has awareness of strengths and weaknesses then these can be used to their advantage or training can be targeted at the weak areas.

Ensure there is a mix of talking to the audience, group discussion, handouts with theory explained for later reading and practical hands-on time. It is useful for participants to be able to practice and try out new techniques learned during the course, as this helps embed what has been learned and also adds variety to the session.

Sometimes the training is explicit – the user presents with a demand for help in how to use a particular tool and sets up a time for a training session. At other times the training methods may have to be much more discrete. Training could be included in answer to a general information query, where a user presents with a specific problem using or accessing a tool or finding information. They want help there and then and they do not see this request for help as a request for training. This is nonetheless an opportunity to deliver some basics while meeting the specific need, or to set up a time for future sessions once the immediate problem or issue has been dealt with.

Use of mind maps

The use of mind-mapping techniques during an IL session is sometimes an effective way of analysing a topic (Webber et al., 2003). A mind map is a visual display of concepts that conform with natural processes of the brain. A diagram is used to represent ideas and topics, which are arranged around one idea. It can be used to help generate search strategies, to capture a lot of information or make decisions on how to organise information.

A project team at Unilever used mind-mapping techniques to gain an overview of their subject interests. This enabled them to prioritise which aspects required further research and analysis (Figure 4.2).

Figure 4.2 Unilever mind map

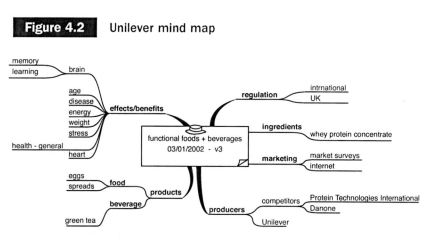

Top Tip

Don't use all your spices in one recipe – combine a few simple flavours. In other words, don't overwhelm your audience.

Presentation

Getting the food out of the kitchen and onto plates (silver service or BBQ?)

It is possible to deliver IL training in a number of ways and you need to decide on the most appropriate method for your customers. Will you deliver to small or large groups? Will this be in a workshop or a more formal setting? Will you use a virtual learning environment or deliver all training face-to-face?

The outcomes of these decisions will be determined by many factors. These factors will vary, but usually include trainer's time for preparation and delivery, the budget you have for the development of course materials, availability of relevant IT equipment (e.g. projectors, PCs, software) and availability of suitable training rooms etc. This of course is never straightforward, and a sensible balance or compromise usually has to be struck. Your customer may demand a two-day feast, but as the sole chef for the company you may only have time to provide a lunchtime buffet.

Consulting your customers about delivery preferences is essential, as is finding out what type of training format is most effective in your particular organisation. As already mentioned, meeting the needs of customers with different learning styles is also important to consider as this will also influence the delivery format you adopt.

Overnight marinade or a quick omelette

Time is usually very precious to your customers within the workplace. There are many steps you can take to maximise their convenience and reduce the time they spend actually training.

Top Tip

Boelens (2001) reported that most of the training carried out in the law firm used in their study was undertaken on a one-to-one or 'just in time' basis. Training could be pitched at the skill level of each individual and they could be taught exactly what they needed to know.

Pack a picnic

Trainers often choose to use standard training rooms to deliver their courses. This approach is usually more advantageous for the trainer as you can usually accommodate large groups and have easy access to essential IT equipment. However, if you are flexible about the location of your training session it may be more beneficial to your customer.

The staff in your organisation may be dispersed across a number of different offices, buildings and perhaps even different sites. If a one-to-one training session is required, consider visiting your customer at their own desk (Bell, 2001). This saves them time and can be more convenient if your customer has locally-stored information they need to show you.

If you want to take a more ad-hoc approach to delivery, think about holding IL 'surgeries' where you invite customers come along with IL-related issues (e.g. how can I retrieve more relevant patents? Which information sources can I use to find out about skin aging? How can best share this information with my team?). These surgeries could potentially be established in communal areas where you are clearly visible, e.g. in staff cafés or reception areas. Visibility also has the advantage of raising your profile (Harrington, 2005).

Top Tip

> At Avecia, the Information Scientist would go to their satellite sites and run regular roadshows for users. These would be followed up with newsletters and e-mail bulletins to keep users connected and in the loop.

There are practical issues to consider with this approach. These are just some of the considerations:

- access to PC or laptop;
- connection to the internal network;
- access to relevant PC drives;
- relevant software availablilty;
- password/access to relevant databases;
- access to the Internet;
- copies of relevant handouts/manuals;
- easy access to training material/examples.

The virtual restaurant

Not all customers will want face-to-face training and may prefer to access training resources independently and in their own time. Developing an e-learning solution addresses this issue. If resources are limited, consider using existing electronic 'information skills' tutorials, such as INFORMS, which can be customised. A VLE, such as Blackboard or WebCT, can be used as a replacement for face-to-face training. However, it is more commonly used to provide trainees with supporting material following on from a course. For example, it may contain quizzes to test new skills, provide copies of presentations, notes, handouts, reading lists etc.

If you work in an organisation with a central training unit, find out if they are using e-learning interactive software. If possible use their resources, experience and knowledge of e-learning design and development.

Top Tip

At Unilever, an IL website was developed primarily to support the IL training programme (Figure 4.3). This is a comprehensive source of information, providing details, examples and links relating to various aspects of IL. Users are advised to dip into the website following on from face-to-face training sessions.

Figure 4.3   Example page from Unilever IL training website

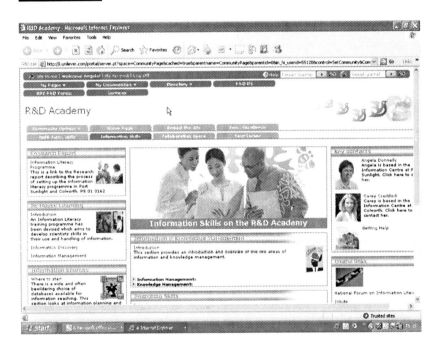

Are your customers hungry?

It has been widely acknowledged that 'information literacy' as a concept is largely unrecognised within the commercial sector (O'Sullivan, 2002). Consider using other labels that appeal to your audience. For example, government IL programmes have been given the label 'working smarter' (Abell, Skelton and Winterman, 2003).

Within the workplace, you will either need to influence stakeholders in order to fund an IL programme (Scammell, 2001) or you will need to continually sell and attract new customers to the IL programme in order to justify its existence. The objectives are therefore to demonstrate the benefits of the IL programme both to the company and to the individual.

Many examples can be found of how the lack of IL skills amongst employees can be detrimental to the company (Cheuk, 2002). Consider 'real' events that have occurred within organisations and that had detrimental results for those organisations due to information being badly handled. Use these to demonstrate the value of IL training. For example:

- A product fault that could be traced back to lack of thorough research – this results in the company losing £2 million. (Key marketing message: adoption of effective searching skills by researchers would have prevented this.)

- A patent application is rejected because a professional prior art search carried out only when requested at the end of the project and not at the beginning has revealed competitor X having intellectual property rights. Three years of project work have been wasted. (Key marketing message: prior art searches should never be carried out by end users using desktop resources. Information professionals should always be consulted, and this should be completed as early as possible in the life of the project.)

Demonstrating the benefits of adopting IL to individuals can also be performed in a similar manner. Remember the 'real' enquiries you have dealt with that have lead to your customer benefiting from IL training. For example:

- An enquirer at the help desk is getting frustrated because they can't find good quality information about how green tea is beneficial to your health. So far they've searched Google and Yahoo! (Key marketing message: having an awareness of more appropriate information sources would retrieve more relevant and peer-reviewed information.)

- Members of separate project teams are working on similar research topics. They discover they are finding and downloading similar documents, which is a duplication of effort. (Key marketing message: using a common place to store key documents, e.g. by use of a shared searchable database, would reduce time wasted and increase project efficiency.)

- A customer tells you that they don't need any help when it comes to information handling. Chances are that they fall into the group of users who 'don't know what they don't know' (Jezzard, 2002). It is always worth gently probing them for more detail on how they find or manage information and diplomatically, and to make suggestions on how this could be undertaken more effectively (and demonstrate this if you can). (Key marketing message: breaking old information habits may enable you to work more efficiently.)

Using quotes from previous participants of courses can be really effective in selling the benefits of your programme. These could be taken from evaluation forms.

Getting the message across...

It is effective to use as many different marketing channels as you can to publicise the IL programme. These may include the use of websites, flyers, e-mail or plasma screens in public areas. Publicising in workplace communal areas is very effective, e.g. the restaurant, coffee areas, notice boards in receptions. Make use of existing routes that publicise other workplace training events (e.g. a training events bulletin published by the Personnel department). It is wise to be sensitive to acceptable level of marketing within the workplace. Colleagues may not appreciate a bombardment of e-mails or leaflets. Choose appropriate marketing channels and be aware of the organisational culture.

Consider ways to personally spreading the message about your IL programme. Attend different workplace events (e.g. internal conferences, team 'away days', or departmental meetings) where you could possibly market your IL programme (Bell, 2001; Harrington, 2005).

Top Tip

> At a large pharmaceutical company, staff from the Information Team will attend other groups' regular meetings in order to publicise new tools or services.

Targeting new employees is also an effective way to attract customers to your programme. If the information unit has an induction programme, include some publicity about IL and take the opportunity to sell its benefits. Approaching new starters a few weeks later to discuss any possible training requirements can also be useful as these are not often identified initially.

Good reports from customers who have been on the course and found it valuable can also be a very powerful medium. If you have one or two who are highly regarded in their areas they can act as ambassadors for the programme and help to spread the word.

Second helpings and repeat customers

It is also worth targeting those who may have been in the organisation for some time and who may feel uncomfortable about requesting updates in their training. Let your customers know that just as the environment in which they operate is fast moving, the same is true of the information world with new tools being developed or rolled out all the time. Roles may have changed and users may suddenly find themselves having to play much more of an active role in information gathering. Some users may also just like to come back again for regular updates or informal discussions about the tools or any techniques they may be struggling with, and it is important that the climate is such that they feel welcome and able to ask for such help.

Top Tip

In Unilever, research is usually conducted within project teams. Effective information handling is important throughout the research cycle. Invariably, large literature or patent reviews will be undertaken to gain knowledge of new science areas. Getting involved with project teams (particularly when this is first established) is an ideal opportunity to market the IL programme and outline how relevant training may help the team. This may include training on the use of relevant information sources, developing current awareness strategies, or managing the team information.

Preparing for and dealing with disasters

It is almost inevitable that something will go wrong on the day but there are a number of steps one can take in order to reduce the likelihood of disasters happening or reducing their impact if they do occur. Preparation is the key, so make sure you are well prepared. Check out web links, take screenshots of key tools and have these on overhead projector slides or as part of your presentation. If you cannot connect to the network or the tool at the time of your session, at least you will still be able to talk your audience through the demonstration. Test all equipment and know who you need to contact if any problems develop during the session – have names and contact numbers to hand.

Ensure your users have realistic expectations before the course starts and check these at the start of the session – what is expected of them and what will and will not be covered. There can be nothing more disconcerting than finding out that your audience is expecting something to be covered for which you are not properly prepared.

If you are demonstrating a database search for a group with a specific subject need, try out examples in advance. Test run your material or any 'new recipes' with colleagues if possible as this will help to iron out or highlight any potential difficult areas.

Finally, never ever panic if things do start to go wrong – this only makes the situation worse!

Compliments to the chef

How can you tell if the meal has been a success? It is very hard to measure the actual impact in terms of altered behaviour, however it is important to be able to demonstrate not only to those who have taken time out to attend the course, but to your sponsors, that they have had value for money. The pilot course at Unilever was evaluated as part of a final MA in Librarianship thesis by Patrick Green from Sheffield University in 2000 (Green, 2000).

Green interviewed all of the participants who attended the first course one week after they had attended. He found that participants had found the discussions to be the most valuable part of the course. Although some of them had felt they already had quite good searching skills, all felt they had learned something new to make their searching even more effective. They also felt that the insights they had gained into their team – both from ways of working and tools being used to the types of search being carried out – were very useful and could help reduce duplication of effort and make them more effective as a team.

An immediate way to measure effectiveness is to get participants to run searches before and after the course and compare the results to see if they are more effective when they are repeated using new techniques learned (Bawden and Robinson, 2002; Donnelly and Craddock, 2002). End users also report that the results they obtain after training are of a better quality and this could in part be due to the increased use of quality databases rather than reliance on Internet search engines. It has also been noted in all the organisations contacted where training is being offered that training delivered by information professionals with subject expertise appears to be the most beneficial.

Increased requests for passwords to access databases could also be seen as a measure of success, as could requests for follow up sessions focussing on new tools. Evaluation forms can also provide useful feedback and can be a good source of quotes that can then be used to market the course as well as make any changes if required.

In the longer term success is more difficult to measure, but in general it is found that as more users undergo training there are less users who present with basic problems at the enquiry desk. Users seeking help from specialists are found to have conducted much more effective initial searches on the appropriate databases. Lastly, when users move into new areas where there may be unfamiliar tools they present for training on these much earlier than they would previously have done.

Finally though, one of the easiest ways to evaluate the immediate impact of your training is to see how your customers look as they leave – are they happy and smiling? Do they seem enthused by what they have just learned or do they just look bewildered and exhausted? This is often the quickest way to get immediate feedback.

Top Tip

> A quote from a Unilever customer
> The IL programme has '...obviously made my searches more specific and has reduced the time sat in front of the terminal. Overall it has made me more inclined to search for information and to persevere with the computer....So in brief, it has changed the way I search for information, and I think that is for the better. Thank you once again for your time and enthusiasm.'

Sample menus

Starters

Invite all new starts by personal e-mail to a brief 45 minute introduction, at a mutually convenient time, to the tools and services offered by Information Services during their first two weeks if possible. This is accompanied by an open invitation to come back once work plans and roles are clarified in order to focus on the areas that would be most useful.

A la carte

Designed for project teams who select areas they feel they need to cover as a team – usually new teams starting to work together who feel they will benefit not only from the topics covered in the session but also gain greater insight and understanding to the way they work as individuals and where they can leverage skills to work more effectively as a team. Teams who choose this option cover not only the theory but also work on practical real-life information requirements, so they go away with some tangible output relevant to their project.

Typical menu items include:

- Defining the concepts:
  - what is information?
  - what is data?
  - what is knowledge?
  - the information cycle.
- Learning styles – understanding own and those of team.
- Audit of tools/sources being used in the team to identify any gaps.
- Clarifying the question – what is it you need?
- Universal principles for developing a search strategy:
  - Boolean operators;
  - synonyms;
  - truncation and character substitution.
- Advanced principles for developing more complex strategies:
  - proximity operators;
  - nested searching;
  - concept grids;
  - mind mapping;
  - thesauruses;
  - fielded searching.
- Source selection: detailed information on the sources available and advice on how to select the most appropriate one for the search
- Source evaluation:
  - Internet;
  - desktop tools.
- Are you legal? A look at information policies:
  - copyright;
  - internal information security policy.

- Managing information:
  - What tools are available and what is your team using?
  - Does your team have a strategy for managing information?
- Sharing information:
  - publishing internally;
  - publishing externally;
  - patenting.

Fast food

A short one hour session covering the 'universal principles' and applying these to a tool that the enquirer has identified as one they need to use in order to conduct their research, and if appropriate introducing a new tool the user may not be familiar with but which would meet their needs better.

Coffee and petit fours

The authors would like to thank to the following people who spoke to us and provided valuable insights for the chapter:

Aart van den Kuilen, Senior Information Specialist, Solvay Pharmaceuticals B.V.; Pam Toplis, Scientific and Patent Information Specialist, formerly of Avecia and now of Serengeti Information Services; Anna Wesson; Madeleine Tseyoungsun, Branch and Group Coordinator, CILIP; Sheila O'Flynn, Independent Information Specialist, InfoValues, Cork, Ireland.

We would also like to thank all staff in the Information Centres within Unilever R&D in the UK, the Netherlands and the USA for their support.

Further information: IL resources

Information literacy general

CILIP Information Literacy Special Interest Group:
http://www.cilip.org.uk/specialinterestgroups/bysubject/informationliter acy/default.htm
Information literacy publications, training events and conferences.

Information Literacy:
http://www.informationliteracy.org.uk/
Blogs, case studies, publications, events, IL resources.

Information skills courses

TFPL:
http://www.tfpl.com/index.cfm

ASLIB:
http://www.aslib.co.uk/training/

CILIP:
http://www.cilip.org.uk/training/

Information literacy discussion list

http://www.jiscmail.ac.uk/lists/LIS-INFOLITERACY.html

References

Abell, A., Skelton, V. and Winterman, V. (2003) 'A new kind of worker', *Library and Information Update*, 2(10): 38–9.

Bawden, D. and Robinson, L. (2002) 'Promoting literacy in a digital age: approaches to training for information literacy', *Learned Publishing*, 15(4): 297.

Bean, W.R. (2001) 'Information literacy: requirements of the 21st century workplace', *Journal of Instruction Delivery Systems*, 15(2): 14–16.

Bell, F. (2001) 'Marketing the information service', in A. Scammell (ed) *Handbook of Information Management*. London: ASLIB.

Boelens, G. (2001) *Legal Research Skills Education Based on the Principles of Information Literacy: a Re-evaluation for the 21st Century*. Rivers of Knowledge, Proceedings of the 9th Specials, Health and Law Libraries Conference 26–29 August 2001, Melbourne.

British Library (2003) *Guide to Libraries in Key UK Companies*. London: British Library.

Bruce, C.S. (1999) 'Workplace experiences of information literacy', *International Journal of Information Management*, 19(1): 33–47.

Cheuk, B. (2002) 'Information literacy in the workplace context: issues, best practices and challenges', white paper prepared for UNESCO, the US National Commission on Libraries and Information Science and the National Forum on

Information Literacy for use at the Information Literacy Meeting of Experts, Prague, The Czech Republic.

Donnelly, A. and Craddock, C.E. (2002) 'Information literacy at Unilever RD', *library and Information Update*, 1(9): 40.

Gasteen, G. and O'Sullivan, C. (2000) 'Working towards an information literate law firm', in C. Bruce, P. Candy and H. Klaus (eds) *Information Literacy Around the World*. New Zealand: Charles Sturt University; pp. 109–120.

Green, K.P. (2000) 'Assessing the impact of an information literacy programme given to Unilever Research scientists', MA thesis, University of Sheffield.

Harrington, J. (2005) 'Get out of your office and practice in-your-face marketing', *Information Outlook*, 9(2): 19–20.

Heinstrom, J. (2005) 'Fast surfing, broad scanning and deep diving – the influence of personality and study approach on students' information seeking behavior', *Journal of Documentation*, 61(2): 228–247.

Honey, P. and Mumford, A. (1992) *The Manual of Learning Styles*, 3rd edn. Maidenhead: Peter Honey Publications.

Jezzard, H. (2002) 'The pulse', *Information World*, 176: 1–2.

Kirton, J. and Barham, L. (2005) 'Information literacy in the workplace', *Australian Library Journal*, 54(4): 365–76.

Lloyd, A. (2003) 'Information literacy: the meta-competency of the knowledge economy? An exploratory paper', *Journal of Library and Information Science*, 35(2): 87–92.

Lustig, J. (2006) 'TrendAlert: scientists as information users – are they being served?', *Outsell*, 9: 1–15.

O'Sullivan, C. (2002) 'Is information literacy relevant in the real world?', *Reference Services Review*, 30(2): 7–14.

Oman, J.N. (2001) 'Information literacy in the workplace', *Information Outlook*, 5(6): 23–43.

Orna, E. and Stevens, G. (1995) *Managing Information for Research*, 1st edn. Oxford: Oxford University Press.

Reid, C.D., Thompson, J. and Wallace-Smith, J. (2006) 'Impact of information on coporate decision making: the UK banking sector', *Library Management*, 19(2): 86–109.

Scammell, A. (2001) *Handbook of Information Management*. London: ASLIB.

TFPL (1999) *Skills for Knowledge Management: Building a Knowledge Economy*, 1st edn. London: TFPL.

Thompson, J.E. and Cronje, J. (2001) 'A dynamic model of information literacy acquisition', *Mousaion*, 14(2): 3–14.

Webber, S., O'Flynn, S., Johnston, B. and Dale, A. (2003) 'Information: it's all in the mind', *Library and Information Update*, 2(4): 30–4.

Wesson, A. (2006) *Information Literacy in the Workplace*. London: University College London.

Winkler, S. (2001) 'The whys and wherefores of information literacy', *Journal of Instruction Delivery Systems*, 15(2): 25–30.

Alone in the kitchen: when you're the only one providing the service

Sarah Hinton, Manage5Nines Ltd.

This chapter looks at the information literacy (IL) skills of the solo information professional in the context of their everyday working life. The solo is the all-rounder of the information world, providing a complete information service without the support of a team. However, it is important to note that the solo's life should not be a lonely one. Bringing an information-literate service to the customer's table requires communication skills that portray someone who, although working ostensibly on his or her own, is approachable and sociable and well able to transfer searching skills to others through a variety of training methods. This involves a lot of communication with customers and networking with fellow professionals.

Preparation

Information literacy requires back-up from other skills and co-operation from your users, in order to be most effective.

As a solo, your skills can be easily hidden from your users. Do your customers and potential customers know what you do? After all, there is no point in being brilliant at searching if no one knows that you are!

- **Make sure your role is clear.** This applies both to you and your line manager. Often a solo's line manager is someone who may not understand very well what the job involves. A well-defined job specification helps to explain this and should be approved and understood by your line manager.

- **Advertise your skills and services.** For your users and customers, producing leaflets, brochures, and maintaining an information services page on a company intranet are all good ways of advertising and describing your role and how you can help people find what they need.

- **Time management.** The solo needs excellent time management skills, as there is no assistant. Always ask your enquirer what the timescale is for a search, or how long they want you to spend searching (this also helps if you need to (re)charge for your time).

- **Organisational knowledge.** This helps you to be proactive. The more you know about the aims and objectives of your organisation and how its staff function, the better your searches and proactive services will be. If you take the trouble to get to know your users and talk to them, you will gain an understanding of their specialisms and professional interests. You will start being able to forward items of interest to them without them having to ask. This is described in the jargon, as 'pushing' information to users, or SDI – selective dissemination of information, and, when accurately aimed, always looks particularly impressive! Find out what sort of projects are going on and, at the same time, the organisation will learn about how you work. Colleagues are then far more likely to volunteer information to you, which is especially vital for a solo.

- **Allies and information champions.** The solo should aim to have allies within the organisation. These people will champion your services and remember (on your behalf) that you exist. So when a colleague mentions a problem or topic that you could contribute to (for example, which source to use for a particular search, or information issues such as knowledge management) they will point them in your direction. Find and foster these people by sitting with them at lunchtime and attend other social functions when the opportunity arises. This sort of informal networking can be very informative, as well as anecdotally entertaining. During one such lunchtime with consultant colleagues we ended up covering the Wikipedia, Creative Commons, and the future of free and priced information! Time is valuable and of course you don't have to go to every social event, but make the effort to join in now and then and/or take on another role in the company where you can interact with others (for example, my own is as 'travel for work and cycling' representative).

- **Make sure you are on relevant e-mail lists.** These let you know what's happening around the company. After a little while you will be able to select the best ones to remain on so that you don't get swamped with e-mails. You may well start out as a passive reader, but then find that you start contributing to the lists when you can answer someone's question. This adds to your visibility, reminding people that you are there with searching skills to offer.

Ingredients in the store cupboard

Know your sources

Be very competent at searching what you currently use and adventurous in exploring new and unfamiliar sources

Keep yourself up to date with new sources by taking free trials or having demonstrations of any that look worthwhile and relevant to your work. This can also provide a way to hone your search skills as you get the chance to investigate an unfamiliar tool. This will develop your understanding of the more subtle aspects of how sources covering similar types of information differ in their provision and structure.

Attend training courses or online training sessions when subscribing to a new resource. Even if you are familiar with similar platforms, a new one will differ enough to warrant the time taken to have more formal training offered by the provider. This initial training, given by an expert, will benefit you by saving time in future as you will learn how to search the resource in the most effective manner. Such training also tends to be provided for free, once you have subscribed. Additionally, watching other people present training helps you to train others better, as you can pick up tips and techniques.

Some companies offer to come and help you run on-site training courses, which can be very useful, not least because it gives your users someone else to listen to. However, be aware that these trainers often begin with a set introductory script that can take up to 10 minutes before they even touch upon how to search their product. It's a good idea to ask them politely to keep brief the inevitable 'how the company began' and 'we're better than our rivals because...' sales patter!

Discuss sources with your users. Ask if they are already familiar with any sources from previous jobs, or if they have any favourites that they find particularly helpful. It is also sometimes useful to know how much access to information they had at their previous work place. Some users have to go through their information unit for searches on specialist or priced sources, others have access at their desktops and will ask the information professional for guidance in how best to go about a search as often as they will ask for a search to be performed for them. Where this is the case, it can be helpful to invite selected users to join you in evaluating information sources. You will learn more about your users and their information needs and it always helps the solo to have another opinion. Your users can learn valuable information literacy tips from seeing you asking key questions about:

- **Currency.** How often is the source updated?

- **The authority of the data.** Where does it come from? Some third-party supplied databases ask the companies themselves to provide the data, others gather it themselves. The latter method can add more value and prove more reliable and consistent content, especially for company databases. The book *The Skeptical Business Searcher* provides a wealth of information about assessing the authority of web-based sources.

- **Coverage and general scope of the source.** Some sources aim to be comprehensive, others focus on a sector or geographic region. How much detail do the records provide and does this level of detail vary from record to record? Company databases tend to vary in how much information is provided depending on whether the companies are private or not.

- **Value add.** Does the source give you information that you wouldn't find for free by searching the Internet? Although with subscription business news databases a proportion of the information will consist of articles that can be found for free on the web, there should also be a good amount of data that would not be so readily available. It is not really acceptable to have a source that sells itself primarily on the pretext of putting lots of information in one easy to find search interface. Harder to find or subscription data must be included too.

- **The search interface.** This needs to be easy to use, especially if your users will also have access at their desks, but with enough functionality to allow more than basic searching. Is Boolean searching supported? This is often seen as a rather old-fashioned question usually only asked by information professionals, but it still has its place. Ask about the indexing behind the database and aspects such as word-stemming, truncation and proximity indicators.

- **Downloading options.** Can records be downloaded in Excel or .csv formats? Is there a limit to the number of records that can be downloaded?

- Try to have an **example of your own ready to try out**. This is always preferable to just relying upon the sales representative's stock search example that, understandably, will be designed to bring back a good result.

- **Pricing formats.** Many sources offer a variety of options such as pay as you go, or a single up-front payment. Find out whether subscription levels are dependent upon usage-levels or the number of people accessing the source. Does downloading incur extra costs, such as credit units?

- **Who do they consider their rivals to be?** I tend to ask this question casually towards the end of a demonstration. Why would you ask this? There are several reasons, apart from giving you the names of competitor products! It is handy to get an idea of how open the company is to discussing the competition, which in itself may reveal a little about their confidence in their own product. It indicates where the company is positioning itself in the market and hints at how well the company know their market or potential rivals.

Equipment

A good computer and the right supporting software is essential. If you can cultivate good relations with the IT department, it will work to your mutual advantage. I work alongside, and with, our IT department, so they have gradually gained a good understanding of what I do and vice versa. Solos can gain a lot by using the overlap in the two professions to their advantage. Information professionals are well placed to work with IT in evaluating desktop search tools, enterprise searching tools or helping to design the intranet. CILIP's UK e-Information Group (*http://www.ukeig.org.uk*) is a useful group to join for getting to grips with some of the IT behind searching tools. In addition to a newsletter, the group also runs workshops covering topics such as desktop search tools, managing e-book collections and knowledge management.

Explore up and coming sources such as blogs, Wikis and RSS newsfeeds. Communities like Freepint and the UK Electronic Information Group, UKeiG, provide articles and courses that will help you understand and make the most of new media.

Top Tip

Keep up to date with freely available e-mail newsletters, such as:

- BestBizWeb Eletter – *http://www.bestbizweb.com*, Information Today
- Freepint – *http://www.freepint.com*
- Google's 'Tips of the Trade'
- Mary-Ellen Bates' Search Tip of the Month
- ResearchBuzz, Tara Calishain – *http://www.researchbuzz.com*
- SearchDay – *http://www.searchday.com*
- Tales from the Terminal Room, RBA Information Services – *http://www.rba.co.uk*
- VIP, also from Freepint

Method: who's doing the cooking – you, your enquirer or both?

It is a truth universally acknowledged, by the information profession, that what someone at first says they need to find, usually turns out to be quite different in the end. (With apologies to Jane Austen!)

How to make sure you have understood the recipe and been given the right instructions.

This is known in the trade as 'the reference interview' and I cannot over-emphasise the importance of using this skill. This is the technique that enables you to carry out searches across specialist areas without having the relevant degree. There will always be some searches that really do require in-depth subject knowledge, but not very many! Being no chemist, I have had clients doubt my ability to carry out a chemistry-based search, only to find that, after diligent questioning, I have been able to find what's required after all, much to the surprised delight of the client. I'll admit that I still end up a little surprised, myself, at how effective this can be!

This type of detective work can be tricky and is often a step-by-step process, so you may well go back to the user with further questions several times. Getting to the point where you feel satisfied that you have as much information about a search as can be provided sometimes takes a fair amount of determination. Most searches require you to ask questions of the enquirers to find out if what they say they are looking for is the same as what is really required.

When I was just starting out as a solo, I found that a key factor was to conquer the feeling that I'd be giving my customers the impression that I was stupid if I had to go back to ask questions about a search more than once. On the contrary, it is only with basic enquiries or very forthcoming, enlightened users that you are likely to manage to get a clear picture of the true needs of the search in one go. To begin with, you may not know what questions you should be asking. I've frequently found that I can only begin to get a more detailed idea of what else I need to know by starting on a search.

Interviewing techniques and questions you can use in order to get clarification:

- Ask how recent the information needs to be.

- What is the geographic coverage: UK, Europe, global?

- What is it for? Try to get some context by finding out about the story behind the request. Some enquirers simply don't think you need to know this, and if confidentiality is an issue then this may be insurmountable, but context gives you an understanding of how the information is going to be used and by whom, versus the enquirer's perception – after some discussion, you may both agree that the search details need to be amended.

- Has the enquirer given you all the information they have? This is a particularly common problem for all types of searches. What does the company make? Is it private or a subsidiary? For patents, does the enquirer have an assignee, inventor names, any other reference numbers? What is it about? If you need more information, check and re-check with your enquirer. Vital little details are so often withheld as they seem irrelevant to your enquirer, who may think the company name or some variant of patent number is enough, but a bit more digging often unearths the key to a successful search result.

- For unclear requests, it helps to ask for an idea of what an ideal search result would look like.

- What, if any searching, has the enquirer already carried out, and which sources were used? This is very relevant for the solo's environment, where users also often have access to business information sources at their desktops.

- If the enquiry is very vague, a helpful tactic is to carry out a quick initial search, and give the results to your enquirer asking whether you are on the right lines. This gives the enquirer a basis upon which to clarify the search and helps stimulate discussion without you having to second-guess all the questions that you should be asking.

Questions on the information menu: some common and less-common occurrences

- **Very common dish.** Or in other words, there's too much information on the topic. Find out what particular aspects your enquirer wants to know about. If the reply is 'an overview of everything, please, I need to be an expert by tomorrow for a meeting', then suggest a taster of all the main aspects, which can include: market overview, major players, key patents, latest research, up and coming technologies and general commentary on current and future trends.

- **Obscure ingredients.** Are you expected to find an answer, or prove that there isn't one? Sometimes a user will want independent confirmation about something for which they already have the answer, or will be seeking to demonstrate how little information is available. In such situations, you will not be cheating if you ask for some idea of what they are expecting you to find or even if they are expecting you to find anything at all. For example, having asked these questions, I've been told that the results should bring up articles by a specific author, or that they would expect me to find very little freely-available information on the topic in question.

- **Has your enquirer already started searching?** If your users like searching for themselves, it is important to avoid duplication of effort. It may be that they are just having trouble finding one particular bit of information.

- **Costs.** Can you give your enquirer an estimate of the likely cost? Conversely, can the enquirer tell you how much you can spend? Can you purchase information, or are you expected to glean as much as you can from free sources? If you need to charge for your time, state this clearly. It is easier if this is advertised as part of your overall service policy, although you may still have to remind enquirers from time to time.

- **Which source to search.** Some enquirers start their question with 'could you do a quick Google search to find out xxxx'. Answer: not necessarily. Use the method that will help you best to find information: online search, sending an e-mail enquiry, phoning, talking to colleagues, suggesting borrowing a book on the topic and so on.

- **Too much to take in.** How much information is required? A few users like mounds of information to plough through, but most don't have the time for this. To avoid overloading your enquirer, keep reminding yourself of what the search is about. Re-read the enquiry so that your searching remains relevant.

- **Explaining the strategy and results.** Sometimes, especially if the search has been obscure or very tricky, it helps to outline your search strategy to your enquirer, highlighting the constraints or limitations. For example, finding market information on a very niche industry area may be possible, but only by purchasing an expensive market report. Finding someone well-versed in the industry to speak to can provide an alternative option, e.g. a magazine editor, industry association, or one of the main companies in the sector.

- **Serving complex or tricky search results.** Sometimes you will want to do more than just present search results to your enquirers. Talking through your findings and how you searched with your enquirer face-to-face, or by phone or e-mail if the search is more of a 'take-away' enquiry, can be mutually beneficial. It gives you a chance to qualify what you have found or had trouble finding.

- **Unclear enquiries.** Even with the best reference-interviewing skills, some enquiries are simply vague. It may be that the customer isn't quite sure what they are looking for. If you are unsure whether what you are finding is relevant or what the next step is, try to work more closely with your enquirer. Don't be afraid to present some interim results to check that you are on the right lines, or to invite them to sit with you while you search. This educates your users in how complex some searches can be. Never plough on in silence in the vague hope that some of what you find will be OK. This is almost bound to result in information that is off-target, resembles a burnt offering, or the output being returned to the kitchen to be re-made.

Are you just supervising the search?

Is your enquirer a savvy searcher? I work with several colleagues who are well-versed in searching their own area of expertise.

As all my colleagues have access to search tools at their desktop, many already have, or expect to gain, a reasonable level of IL. Some like to be fairly independent, using me as a back-up for really awkward searches or ones that they need to share out (they allocate various aspects of the search to me, searching on the remainder themselves). These people need to be well-versed in searching across a range of resources, such as:

- patent databases;
- market and news research;
- company data;
- academic literature searches;
- general web searching.

Although a good number of people always sign up for the more formal group sessions that I have arranged, due to the type of work it is very hard for users reliably to commit their availability in advance. All too often, client meetings crop up at short notice or project-work needs to be urgently completed. As a result I end up with about six people attending and an e-mail inbox full of apologetic messages.

Therefore, for those that are keen to search, one-to-one training sessions seem to be the most effective rather than organising a formal group session. Even so, I will organise group training when introducing a major new resource to my users. It is important to be prepared to provide on-the-job IL training at short notice, as and when required. For each search tool, work out a simple training structure that can be easily repeated, or use a crib-sheet listing the points you need to cover.

If you don't already know how information literate your user is, it is well worth asking a few questions to find out. This sort of training can easily be pitched to the level of the individual's IL ability, is a timely way of helping self-service users learn to use a specific source properly, and gives you the opportunity to share your expertise. An added advantage is that the search strategy and/or search terms are usually based upon a real enquiry, and therefore of maximum relevance to the user, which also encourages maximum concentration from your user!

Some examples of the points that I would look to include in an IL session are provided below. However, it is important to note that I always stress that though self-searching is an option, I am always on hand to carry out searches. I am keen to avoid any misunderstanding that users are *obliged* to do their own searches!

Top Tip: information literacy training on the go

Part of IL training is about managing expectations. Effective searching requires a good understanding of what a search tool is designed to be used for, together with its limitations.

At times, I've found users complaining that they are 'disappointed' with a source because it won't allow searching or provide results in the particular way that the user would like. Upon asking what they are trying to do, I often discover that the search they are trying to run is quite demanding and simply unsuitable for that particular database, and so not really a failure of the source itself. In the case of company databases, for example, the problem is usually that the complexity of the search demands a much greater level of detail that is available using SIC or NAICs codes, and would therefore require a more specialist resource focussing on a group of sectors, such as the CorpTech company database, which covers US technology companies (*http://www. corptech.com*).

Company searching. Give the user an overview of the best sources to use. Cover how to search both private and public companies and explain why it can be hard to get data on private companies. I outline the main sources I use, their strengths and weaknesses, and any cost implications.

Market research. As above, I go through the various major sources that can be used, then, taking the main source we subscribe to, I take the user through a search to show how to use the tool most effectively, making sure to highlight any less-obvious aspects of the search interface. I also explain what they can expect to find for free, such as top-level market sizes, via general web-based or news searching and what is more likely to be unavailable unless paid for (e.g. niche markets or industries that tend to keep their market data quite confidential). We also look at some sample results – unless it costs to download!

Patent searching. This is usually more specific to the source subscribed to by an organisation. Therefore, the search tends to be

Top Tip continued

based mostly around a single source. However, I also highlight sources like Espacenet (*http://ep.espacenet.com*) as it now provides free downloads for almost all patents in pdf format. Also, for obscure patent searches (for example, Korean patents) it is usually worth searching for the patent office or database provided by the country concerned, as they may provide more data than the all-encompassing databases.

Academic literature. Here, we use a mixture of free and subscription databases. Science search engines like Scirus and Google Scholar can be very effective. I usually only need to demonstrate Scirus (*http://www.scirus.com*) as my users are familiar with Google searching. Depending on the budget available, the user may also want to search priced databases, in which case I give them an overview of the best interface we use to access these databases and make it very clear how much searching and downloading is likely to cost.

News research. This is very popular among my self-service users and can also help with searching for information on all the above. My training tends to follow much the same pattern as for market research and will also highlight how to search across selected sources and how to use the search interface to the best advantage. This is important with users who can get rather used to solely entering a few keywords in Google without looking at the other options a specialist resource may offer, such as industry, source, language, geographic area and context.

When training, it is necessary for the trainer to be prepared to answer questions like 'why do we subscribe to Source X rather than Source Y?'. The reasons usually include the cost and content coverage.

Mediated searches, quick reference guidance and marketing

By contrast, some users are not interested in self-service searching and prefer to have mediated searches instead. For these users, there is less IL training to be given, but it is worth them knowing what sort of searches can be carried out and the sorts of sources. They still need to have a clear understanding of what you do, otherwise they may not ask for help.

Below are some options of how to reach these users while also ensuring that all users have some level of IL. These also serve as marketing tools and can raise your profile within the organisation quite effectively.

- Send out concise 'search tips' e-mails. Tips e-mails tend to get read by most people because of the aim of their format: to be brief, to the point and relevant. I receive very positive feedback from users whenever I send out this type of IL e-mail. They generally consist of a combination of alerting users to new websites, an improvement to a specific search resource or a handy search tip. The end of the e-mail always states to users, 'don't hesitate to ask if you have any questions'.

- Current awareness by e-mail. Again, you are providing very targeted and relevant information to a user or group of users that gives them something to help them in their work, while at the same time giving an example of why you are so useful.

- Produce 'How to find…' quick reference guides on specific topics such as those listed in the box above. I produce these as a downloadable A4 brochure, but you can use any combination you wish as long as it is clear and easy to read. List relevant sources, and maybe also ones to avoid. Include search techniques, such as phrases or terms to use, for example how to search for numerical ranges on Google. Highlight what information may be found for free, versus what will be harder to find or will be priced. Tailor the guide to your users so that it matches the resources they have access to. You can make these smart, with a company logo or your own information services logo, but always include your contact details and date the guide or give it a version number. This enables you to update the guide easily and to check that users have the latest edition.

The only downside is that you might generate rather a lot of extra work for yourself, at least in the short term, which can make life even more hectic than usual!

Top Tip

> Downloading lists of information from webpages can be difficult to achieve neatly. Cutting and pasting information into a spreadsheet can sometimes result in a mess of information that would require hours to tidy up. Some web browsers have built in features to help with this. The Opera browser (*http://www.opera.com*), available as

Top Tip continued

a free download, provides a 'notes' facility into which selected sections or entire pages can be copied for future reference. The link to the original page is also retained.

Dealing with disasters

Although solos work alone, and need to be highly self-motivated, we are neither loners nor independent of the organisation. We rely on networking within the organisation and outside it. We use support services ourselves and find that a motivational helping hand now and then is very welcome, especially when things go wrong.

- So much information is electronically generated that computer failure, systems crashing and power-cuts can all have a big and immediate impact upon our work. For the solo, this can mean that the whole service is affected, as there aren't any other team members' computers to turn to when yours fails. If you have a good relationship with the IT department, you will have a mutual appreciation that both IT and Library services provide important support services to the whole organisation and this can encourage them provide you with a better service in an emergency.

- Know who to contact when your online sources don't work. In most cases, the customer support helpdesk will be adequate to solve problems, but occasionally, for urgent action, it helps to speak directly to your account manager. Keeping up to date telephone numbers for all your key account managers enables direct conversation, which is much speedier in providing a solution and less frustrating than trying to explain a problem via e-mail and the ensuing suspense of awaiting a response.

Making a significant mistake

Solos are not infallible, and at some point everyone will experience the horrible realisation that they've made a mistake with an enquiry. The thing that can make this situation worse for a solo is that you have no fellow professional at hand to turn to for immediate help. Interestingly, it is worth noting that it may not always be your own error that you are dealing with – a very anxious user may also come to you after having made a search-related mistake.

When something's gone more than a little wrong, contrary to this book's title, making more of a meal of things than you have to is exactly what you want to avoid doing! Damage limitation is needed, usually along with a serving of honesty.

The initial reaction upon discovering a sizeable mistake is usually a sense of alarm, followed by a stomach-churning feeling of panic. Before running to the client to confess all, it is worth taking time to check that you understand where you have gone wrong. It is important that you are clear about this, be it that you – or your anxious user – totally ran out of time, searched for the wrong thing, incurred a huge online cost by downloading 200 full records from an expensive database when intending only to use the free format, or missed out a whole part of a search.

Your IL skills will leave you if you can't think rationally. Make a cup of tea, take a walk around the building, do whatever it takes to calm yourself enough to think clearly, then begin to examine the reasons and implications for what has happened.

- **Be clear on what has happened.** If one of your users has made the error, show concern, but not horror, try to provide some reassurance (but only use humour if you're sure they'll find it funny too) and then ask questions to make sure that you've got all the facts.

- **Re-read the original enquiry.** Were some vital details not given to you? If so, find out what you really should have been searching for.

- **Check the search strategy and sources that were used.**

- **Estimate any cost implications.** This might be all too clear for an erroneous download!

- **Honesty.** If the mistake can't be rectified easily, it is always best – and probably unavoidable – to come clean and tell the client. Trying to cover up for yourself, or on behalf of anyone else, is always unwise and will make things harder later on if a client finds out for himself that something went wrong.

- **Suggest a solution.** In advance of the meeting to explain what has happened, think of what action might need to be taken to rectiofy matters or some possible ways of tackling the problem. This shows your client that you have begun to think beyond the mistake itself and will help focus the discussion onto what to do for the best, rather than unproductively dwelling on the error.

- **For mistaken downloads, check with the information provider about the possibility of getting a refund.**

- Find out if more time can be made available in order to revise or re-do the search.

- Last, but not least, try not to feel too bad or lose confidence. Remember that everyone makes mistakes; it is how they are dealt with that singles out the competent professional from the amateur.

Coffee and petit fours

The dream kitchen

Being a solo information professional should be extremely rewarding: you have to carry the responsibility that comes with being in charge of a department, but you may also enjoy a great measure of autonomy – i.e. having the whole kitchen to yourself!

- Your customers know who did the searching, so your IL skills are highly visible. However, be aware that your organisation also influences how you work, how big your budget is, and probably even where you sit and how much space you have. These aspects will all have an impact on your searching.

- If you are practising good time management, but still find yourself always under pressure and short of time, remember that you can only do the work of one person. Try to avoid getting into the habit of working all hours to compensate, but make your line manager aware, otherwise your organisation will only assume you are fine.

- Work on your reputation, and actively seek feedback from your users. It is important to know your searches are on target, and that what you provided was useful and relevant. You need feedback in order to improve and fine-tune your searching skills to the needs of your users. Most of the time enquirers readily provide thanks or volunteer their feedback having read the search results or at the end of a project, but others will be too busy to remember to acknowledge the value of your contribution. Feedback is especially important for complex searches, or those where the enquiry was vague. You can follow up on searches by sending an e-mail to check that your user received all that was needed or mention the search when you next meet the enquirer if possible, be it a chance meeting in the corridor or when discussing another search request.

- Involve your users in the service you provide. Sometimes my users e-mail me with a site or source that might be of interest. With good information literacy awareness, you should find that 95 per cent of the time they haven't alerted you to anything that you haven't already seen, but it is especially important for solos to welcome help and encourage users to feed them information on any sites and sources that they have found interesting. Users will feel valued by you and you will learn more about their work and what interests them.

- Network widely. All the articles and books I have ever read on solo professionals stress this point with good reason. 'Professional isolation' (St Clair, 1992) is a well-known and oft quoted solo disease. The antidote is to network, making the most of training courses, exhibitions, professional groups and committees to swap search tips and find out how other information professionals work.

- Use the advantage of your autonomy, 'as solo librarians, we are in a better position to do our own planning and to arrange our own time than many others' (Ceylan, 2006).

- Broaden your professional horizons, and talk with any information professional, whether they are solos or not, or from a totally different working background. It can be surprising to discover just how many aspects information professionals from diverse backgrounds have in common.

Top Tip

Look out for relevant communities and professional groups to join. They may cater for your subject specialty or focus on solos within the information profession. For the latter, it is worth joining the Special Libraries Association, which has a Solo Librarians Division (*http://units.sla.org/division/dsol/*).

Sample recipe: the induction of new joiners

This is your chance to demonstrate your services and gain a new customer.

Ingredients

- Suitable location. For example: the library, your desk or a meeting room.

- Brochure or other advertising material.
- Computer with Internet access in order to demonstrate online sources.
- Information services website on the intranet (if you have one).
- Tour of the library or information centre (optional – depends if you have one).
- Checklist of core aspects of the service that you need to cover. Other areas may be included or omitted depending upon what is relevant to the person you are inducting.
- Some background knowledge of the new joiner.

Method

It's useful to start off by asking the new joiner a little about themselves, even if you already have an idea of what sort of work they will be doing. For example, what is their specialist area, and have they had access to desktop search tools in previous jobs? This will help show the new joiner that you are interested in them and their individual needs, rather than that they are just another new employee to be processed.

Knowing something about the person also means that you can tailor the induction to suit their IL level and information needs, rather than just running through a set induction process that might otherwise include a lot of irrelevant information, or go over their heads. Some inductions take less time than others.

Don't explain the service too fast; pause now and then to encourage any questions. Although you will have run through inductions frequently, this is the first time they will have heard it.

Your brochure or website should provide your users with an overview of all the major sources that you use, but in an induction, select for demonstration the sources that will be of interest. For example, there is no point showing a new user how to search for patents if he is never likely to need to do so.

It is often worth asking if your user has a search example that you could try out. Sometimes they will volunteer a search enquiry. This can be one of the best ways for you to focus in on relevant search tools in more depth and for them to see the service in action.

Obviously you want to be seen at your best, but induction time is limited, and there is always the mysterious IL phenomenon that any searching suddenly becomes much harder whenever someone is watching over your shoulder. Size up the request quickly and, if necessary, say if you think the search would be best carried out later. You can still outline the strategy you would use to go about the search in the meantime.

At the end of the induction, ask if there are any more questions and emphasise that you don't expect the new joiner to remember everything that they've just heard. If they need to ask for another explanation on any aspect of the service, that is fine.

The idea is to come across as professional, motivated, very information-literate and approachable. This will encourage people to come back to you time and again for help.

Acknowledgements

I would like to thank Blair Brown, Mark Clark, Lyndsay Rees-Jones and my colleagues at Sagentia for their assistance with this chapter.

References

Ceylan, H. (2006) 'Learning in spite of being a solo', *CILIP Update*, Jan/Feb.
Berkman, R. (2004) *The Skeptical Business Searcher*. Medford, NJ: Information Today Inc.
St Clair, G. (1992) *Managing the One Person Library*, 2nd edn. Croydon: Butterworths.

Educating the palate of pupils and teachers: recipes for success in school libraries

Rebecca Jones

Ensuring that pupils learn essential information literacy (IL) skills during their school career is a challenge that faces all school librarians. This chapter provides some sample 'recipes', general principles and hints and tips that show how the librarian can influence policy and practice within his/her school. Examples from practising librarians and from my own experience at Malvern Girls' College (MGC)[1] provide real-life illustrations of IL theory in action. Let's get cooking!

Theoretical models and frameworks: basic equipment

As with cooking equipment, there are many different 'brands' or IL models available to the school librarian.[2] As the IL expert within your organisation you need to assess these models and choose one that will suit the context of your school. The aim is to choose a standard that will guide students through the research process by defining the steps that they need to take to complete effective information retrieval. As common elements are contained within the different frameworks, you may decide to create your 'own brand' version that is tailored to suit your own style and school. Whatever your decision, you need to make sure that you choose a product that you can trust and that will last. IL models include:

The nine question steps

Marland (1984) produced a popular nine-step approach to information literacy in the early 1980s that involves the information seeker asking themselves a series of questions.

1. What do I need to do? (formulate and analyse need)

2. Where could I go? (identify and appraise likely sources)

3. How do I get to the information? (trace and locate individual resources)

4. Which resources shall I use? (examine, select, and reject individual resources)

5. How shall I use the resources? (interrogate resources)

6. What should I make a record of? (recording and sorting information)

7. Have I got all the information I need? (interpreting, analysing, synthesising, evaluating)

8. How should I present it? (presenting, communicating)

9. What have I achieved? (evaluation)

PLUS

The PLUS model incorporates the elements of Purpose, Location, Use and Self-evaluation, and is designed to enable pupils to identify their own information needs through the use of a range of, note-taking, writing and communication skills. The PLUS model seeks to incorporate the key elements of previous models while adding emphasis on thinking skills and self-evaluation. This model provides a framework that both teachers and librarians can use to increase pupils' awareness of the importance of thinking about what they read, view or listen to.

The Big 6

Eisenberg and Berkowitz (2001–2005) developed The Big 6, a meta-cognitive scaffold, or an information problem solving strategy (Table 6.1). It is a widely used approach to teaching information and technology skills. It's a strategy that can be used to tackle a wide range of information-based questions.

Table 6.1	The Big 6			
1. Task definition	1.1 Define the information problem 1.2 Identify information needed	**4. Use of information**	4.1 Engage (e.g. read, hear, view, touch) 4.2 Extract relevant information
2. Information seeking strategies	2.1 Determine all possible sources 2.2 Select the best sources	**5. Synthesis**	5.1 Organise from multiple sources 5.2 Present the information
3. Location and access	3.1 Locate sources (intellectually and physically) 3.2 Find information within sources	**6. Evaluation**	6.1 Judge the product (effectiveness) 6.2 Judge the process (efficiency)

What are the key IL skills?

In order to complete the successful processing of information, pupils need to possess certain key skills. A skills list is useful as it provides you with a set of tangible outcomes for student achievement. Use the IL conceptual frameworks below to guide your selection of the skills that you want your IL programme to deliver:

- information literacy skills;
- question;
- plan;
- identify and evaluate sources;
- analyse and organise key information;
- synthesise and assimilate;
- reflect;
- communicate;
- evaluate.

(Barrett and Douglas, 2004)

Similarly, Dubber (1999) used Marland as a starting point, and interpreted the nine steps into six key skills:

- planning;
- locating and gathering;
- selecting and appraising;

- organising and recording;
- communicating and realising;
- evaluating.

The KS3 strategy identifies 11 competencies that information-literate pupils should be able to achieve. These 'invisible' process skills are framed with teachers clearly in mind and are particularly useful as they are measurable. (DfES, 2004)

Information-literate pupils...

- know which questions are useful to ask;
- are independent readers, skimming and scanning to find what they need;
- know what is relevant, can select and reject information;
- read texts in different ways for different purposes;
- know when they have found enough information;
- make relevant notes and use them to support classwork and homework;
- synthesise and combine information from a variety of sources;
- re-present information coherently, demonstrating understanding and learning;
- evaluate their sources;
- evaluate their work and reflect on their learning.

Top Tip

The analysis of existing IL models lead to the development of the MGC Independent Learning and Information Literacy Cycle (Jones, 2005; Figure 6.1) that was distributed to all departments for discussion, review and subsequent inclusion in to departmental handbooks.

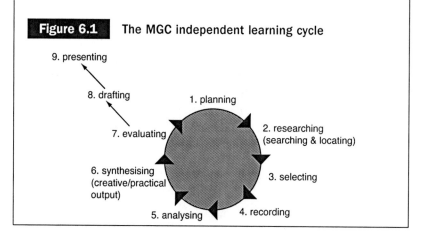

Figure 6.1 The MGC independent learning cycle

9. presenting
8. drafting
7. evaluating
1. planning
2. researching (searching & locating)
6. synthesising (creative/practical output)
3. selecting
5. analysing
4. recording

Top Tip

The result of the IL working group at King Edward VI school, Lichfield resulted in the development of their own in-house brand called BE ALERT; a skills model that aims to modify pupils' researching behaviours:

Before you start
Engage your brain

Ask yourself questions
   What do you need to find out?
Locate the sources
   Remember to use a variety – books (non-fiction and reference) websites, CD Roms, journals, newspapers etc)
Evaluate the sources
   How useful is the information you have found? Is it relevant? Is it reliable? Is it up to date?
Record what you need
   Take notes, save it, print it off, e-mail it home, photocopy pages, highlight important information
Transform

Develop a vision

As the practitioner, you are the most important resource in your library. IL offers you an excellent opportunity to show initiative and provide leadership within an area that has a direct impact on teaching and learning.

Analysis of the theoretical frameworks should enable you to take the first step. The next phase is clear definition of your goals, aims and objectives. This is the stage for clarifying your big ideas, and for menu planning. Look at the overall picture within education, the developments taking place within other schools and the development plans within your own institution. These sources should provide you with vital information about current trends and contexts.

In recent years, the number of advisory documents available to the school librarian has increased. Take advantage of the publications listed and use them to re-enforce yours ideas and plans:

- 'The school library and the Key stage 3 national strategy' (DfES, 2004);
- 'Good school libraries: making a difference to learning' (Ofsted, 2006);
- 'Improve your library: a self-evaluation process for secondary school libraries' (DfES, 2004);[3]
- '14–19 Gateway' (DfES).

Other schools

Gaining a perspective from other school librarians is always useful as their experience can highlight potential pitfalls and also areas of success. Good sources for communication are local SLSs, national organisations such as the SLG or SLA, and CILIP's IL group. The e-mail group SLN is an excellent resource that, due to its diverse membership of both national (UK based) and international librarians, can supply a range of different perspectives and examples.

You will also need to review the development priorities within your own school to identify how your ideas relate to whole-school initiatives. Remember that your ideas are the equivalent of high quality ingredients, but it's no good using them to make a curry if everyone else wants a pizza.

You may need to be creative to link your ideas to a school initiative or you may even have to introduce the theme of IL yourself to even get it put onto the agenda; that is, you may need to persuade your school to try a curried pizza. Finally it's important that you emphasise how your initiatives will improve the quality of learning within the school and how they will benefit the students. Barrett and Douglas' (2004) chapter on information literacy provides a useful list of outcomes relating to good information skills teaching.

Top Tip

> At MGC the librarian used the recommendations from an ISI inspection relating to the development of Independent Learning and linked it with the provision of IL skills in order to spearhead the development of a skills programme within the curriculum.

Share your vision: support is the key ingredient

If you wish to influence whole-school policy then you will need to gain the backing of the management team/governors. Use whole-school and individual departmental documents to link your aims with overall development plans and priorities.

Support is a key issue; if you are to succeed it is vital to get your Head teacher or Principal on your side: '..the most important factor to improvements in school libraries is the commitment and leadership of knowledgeable headteachers...' (Ofsted, 2006; 4).

Presenting your ideas, vision and experiences to managers is essential. You need to sell your case by, explaining how IL can improve learning, demonstrating that IL skills are essential to lifelong learning and showing how IL can become part of raising pupil achievements. The value of a supportive headteacher is summed up in by Ofsted: 'The most effective headteachers had a vision for the library's key role in raising standards and making a difference to learning.' (Ofsted, 2006; 4)

However, do not be discouraged if you are unsuccessful or only partially successful on your first attempt at introducing IL. The most important factor is to be both persistent and determined. Use your meeting to discover whether the Head has any reservations or misconceptions relating to IL and discuss a course of action that you can take to push forward or create an IL agenda for the school. Make sure that you continue to build partnerships within the curriculum so that you can add to your base of evidence.

Once you have convinced the senior managers then it is important to take your message to the teachers, it is these 'cooks' who will be making your IL recipes and serving them to the pupils.

An excellent medium for spreading your ideas is in-service education and training (INSET). Negotiate a timeslot with the Head and use it to, explain key terms, outline your goals and invite discussion and debate. Use the opportunity to ask departments to develop action plans. Formalise the process by including deadlines for departments to submit their plans and arrange follow-up meetings for discussion.

Top Tip

The librarian at the High School of Dundee ran an in-service workshop to staff on Internet search techniques and introduced a set of rules for searching, website evaluation techniques and when to choose an online directory or subject gateway. This resulted in these rules being put into practice and incorporated into lessons delivered by the librarian on e-literacy.

Top Tip

After building up a programme of lessons across the curriculum at MGC, a whole-school INSET session provided the forum for sharing the overall goal for IL skills with the staff. It allowed me to introduce common terminology and raise the awareness of the staff in relation to the work that was taking place within a range of subjects. As I had worked with most of the staff already, the session allowed me to put their lessons into a context. In the next academic year I presented another INSET. This session enabled me to update staff on the progress made with the IL skills programme and also created an opportunity for departments to construct their own IL action plans for the year and submit them to the librarian before half term. This meant that all subject areas had to examine the opportunities that they provided and how they could sustain and/or integrate additional IL skills teaching. Further collaboration was generated as a gap in pupil's ability to plan their research was highlighted and sessions in RS and Chemistry were subsequently devised.

How can you achieve your goals?

Once you have developed your vision the next step is to decide how it can be implemented; are you looking to develop a whole school IL programme, introduce IL to specific subject areas or work across the curriculum within a particular age group or class? Do you want to influence managers or continue to build on relationships with particular teachers?

If you are to convince others, you need to be sure of your own agenda. There are two possible approaches the librarian can either work from the chalk face upwards or start at the top with managers and then disseminate ideas to classroom teachers.

Top Tip

> At MGC, a cross-curricular programme was developed and established before taking the vision to senior school managers. A benefit of developing classroom links first is that it enables the librarian to demonstrate to managers that teaching IL skills within the curriculum is possible within a wide range of subject areas. It also means that the librarian has built up a network of allies who are in a position to develop and discuss improvements to the programme.
>
> A weakness of this approach is that it is time-consuming and hard work to build up trust with individual staff. It also takes a lot of willpower to keep the sessions in place in the face of changing schemes of work and staffing. Only so much can be achieved without having a whole-school framework in place.
>
> At the High School of Dundee the librarian decided to use the fact that there was a gap in IL skill teaching as an impetus for change. The result was that she was asked to chair an IL Working Group and called for interested staff to join.

Stand alone Vs Integrated IL programme

A key issue is whether your IL programme will be served as a main meal, as part of the main curriculum or as a side dish, as a series of lessons that are delivered on a stand-alone basis. The accepted ideal is for IL skills to be taught progressively as an integral part of the curriculum:

> '...the best librarians worked with different subject teachers to teach a coherent and planned programme for IL skills across the curriculum'. (Ofsted, 2006; 19)

> 'IL skills, like all other skills, have the most impact on learning when they are taught, modelled and practised within a meaningful

context. Ideally these skills will be introduced in a developmental progression.' (Barrett and Douglas, 2004; p. 38)

'A key factor in the success of any information skills programme lies in its integration into the school curriculum.' (Herring, 1999; p. 56)

It is important that the skills taught have some practical use for the pupils, and this is best achieved when driven by the content requirements within different subject areas. However, there is a case for providing both types of session as long as the stand-alone training has direct links to the work being undertaken in class and is then reinforced in the classroom, ideally by the librarian.

Top Tip

The note taking lessons that are undertaken with Year 8 pupils at MGC as part of their PSHE programme use techniques that can be referred to, and then used by pupils, in other subsequent lessons across the curriculum. As form staff have a copy of the PSHE timetable and another copy is posted on a board in the staff room, it means that all teachers know when pupils have had a skills lesson. As I team-teach the pupils in different subjects across the curriculum during the term, it means that I can remind them of the techniques that they have learned and form a link between IL skills and subject areas.

It is worth identifying non-examined subject areas or year groups such as PSHE[4] and KS3 lessons as the lack of public examinations can mean that teachers are more willing to incorporate IL opportunities into their lessons.

What skills do you have?

As the librarian, you may find that you are the sole advocate of IL skills within your organisation. You need to be able to negotiate, persuade and communicate ideas to both senior managers and academic staff. Your mission is to persuade teachers to take a risk and trust you to help them integrate IL skills within the delivery of their subject. Use the evidence that you have collected to show teachers how IL skills can enhance the pupils' learning experience and independence. It is important to be very proactive at this stage as in essence you are suggesting that teachers change the way that some of their lessons are delivered, and for some staff this will lead them outside of their comfort zone.

Ensure that you have up to date skills and make sure that you are aware of the technology available in your school (interactive whiteboards, gyro mice, intranets and VLEs). Think about how ICT can be used to enhance your delivery of IL skills training.

Top Tip

> The librarian at Epsom College has utilised technology and integrated it into her teaching. She uses the 'click and reveal' principle on an interactive smartboard to teach the Dewey Decimal system. She has also developed a series of PowerPoint slides on the topic of plagiarism. These resources form the basis of games that are designed to keep pupils focussed when learning IL skills as part of a discrete set of lessons.[5]
>
> At Hurstpierpoint College, the librarian has developed her own Learning Resources section on the school's VLE[6] and, in conjunction with the Physics department, to support their academic week, utilised the quiz function to encourage pupil research by creating two interactive multiple choice quizzes that were advertised to pupils through assembly and also via e-mail. Two hundred pupils took part and their progress was displayed on the electronic scoreboard. After the closing date the librarian ensured that the pupils were able to review their answers using the system. The success of this collaboration has lead to a similar request from the Chemistry department.

If you want to be taken seriously as an educator then you need to have a good knowledge of pedagogy and the different techniques and styles that are employed by a professional teacher. Unfortunately very little professional training relating to teaching is currently available for school librarians; a useful alternative is to arrange teaching observations of your colleagues within your own workplace. This has the twofold benefit of enabling you to observe the teaching methods that they use and how different groups respond, whilst also allowing you to become more familiar with curriculum content.

Store cupboard staples: what resources/facilities do you have?

Resources can be split into three elements: teaching materials, physical and online resources and the actual resource base itself.

The dimensions and equipment within your library will dictate the type and level of service that you are able to deliver. If possible, try to go out into classrooms and ICT suites to deliver IL skills in different contexts. In this way your actual presence can become a physical link to pupils that highlights the transferable nature of IL skills across the curriculum.

Your budget will also affect the level of service that you will be able to provide. If possible use evidence of successful collaborations to argue for additional funding or make joint bids with interested subject areas for additional resources.

Teaching resources

Your level of input into specific lessons will affect the range of resources that you will need to produce. If you are supporting a lesson then this could mean providing access to physical resources, devising help sheets or providing resource guides. This is the traditional support role that the librarian often plays within a school.

If you are team-teaching, then expect to extend a greater input into the planning and delivery of the lesson. Team-teaching requires a high level of confidence from the librarian as not only do you need to be assured in front of the pupils but you also need to feel secure teaching in front of other members of staff. Undertaking lesson observations as suggested earlier is a good confidence builder.

In order to have an effective input into the lesson you need to have a planning session with the subject teacher. In this session you need to understand how the lesson fits into the overall topic, the content that the teacher wants to cover and the amount of time that is available.

Finally, you need to address the issue of cover in the library. Having a library assistant provides the librarian with a greater freedom to attend lessons. If you are a sole practitioner then you will need to discuss this with your line manager and justify your input into the curriculum.

Your profile within the school and your personality

Anne Robinson (School Librarian of the year 2005) said, *'you need to find a way of making yourself indispensable'.*[7] Your personality, as well as your actions, can have a great effect on how you are regarded within your school and more importantly how other staff view your role in relation to teaching and learning.

If you are to push forward your IL agenda then you need to be a visible advocate within your school and actively raise issues of teaching and learning with academic staff and managers. You need self-confidence and self-belief; if staff do not know what you do then make sure you tell them. You can boost your status by, ensuring that senior managers have regular updates on IL, being involved within the curriculum and the life of the school and providing evidence of your impact within the curriculum (as facilitated by the self-evaluation process).

Who can you work with?

It is impossible to work with all the subject areas at once; you will therefore need to select subject areas that lend themselves to the teaching of IL skills, i.e. those subject areas that have projects or research-based topics such as the humanities. Introducing the teaching of skills into these areas is easier as it has a direct link with the delivery of the curriculum.

You need to become the Head Chef and make IL your subject specialism. Once you have formed partnerships encourage staff to tell others – use them as your ambassadors. Provide their department with lots of support and where possible resources and offer to team-teach and deliver IL teaching as the resident expert. Often teachers will appreciate another pair of hands especially if the session involves computers, and you never know, your hard work may be repaid with a 'Michelin star'!

Providing examples for teachers that show them how IL tasks can be integrated into their lessons can help you to recruit new partners, e.g. pupils should always be required to produce a bibliography when they have been set a piece of research, regardless of its length. Explain to the teacher that not only does this train them to record their sources but it also shows the range of resources that the pupil has used. The teacher can then integrate the production of a bibliography into the mark scheme, which in turn provides the student with the impetus to remember to produce it.

Sample recipes: some suggested lessons and ideas

Starters and snacks

- Re-enforcement of key terms from IL cycle:
  - A simple way of raising awareness of IL skills is to ask teachers to discuss IL skills with their class. It could be as simple as asking the pupils which skills they think that they have been using in the lesson or a more formalised written response that can be added to the end of a piece of research.

- Basic rules for Internet searching:
  - Use a simple system like CARS[8] (Harris online) to help pupils evaluate websites. Build in the opportunity for pupils to write a short evaluation of their choice of websites.

- Quick 'find out about' type homework:
  - Advocate the value of quick pieces of research to ensure that pupils have a range of opportunities to practise their skills. Ask pupils to include how long it took them to find the information, as this can be a useful indicator of the skill and difficulty level of the task.

- Library catalogue:
  - Create project specific resource lists and direct pupils towards the catalogue as their first port of call.[9] This is a good way of encouraging pupils to use the library catalogue and you can also use it to ensure pupils use a range of materials and to build in evaluations of selected websites.

- IL games:
  - Short 10-minute games can introduce IL principles to students and be delivered as part of a research lesson.

Mains and 'light bites'

- Projects:
  - Specific collaborations can result in both the librarian's IL agenda and the subject teacher's requirements being met. At MGC a Year 9 PSHE project enabled pupils to learn about different learning styles,

undertake research and present the information they had learned to their peers.[10]

- Short research-based lessons:
  - Quick single-lesson research tasks can enable pupils to practise their selecting and synthesising skills. Pupils are guided towards resources that they have a limited time to interrogate in order to answer key questions, for a subsequent class discussion or as a marked note-taking exercise.

- Independent research:

  - For longer projects, pupils use a pro forma to record the resources that they have used during research sessions that is checked and signed by the librarian as evidence.

Dessert

- Displays:
  - Try to link the IL framework with work that has been produced by pupils as part of a display to raise awareness of IL skills in action both in the library and in classrooms.
- Intranet/network resources:

  - Create a Library area on the school network and post up useful 'Hints 'n' tips' sheets for pupils and staff covering key sources and IL skills. Refer to these resources in lessons and advertise them to staff.
- Use tutor/form time to quiz students:

  - Ask tutors to test pupils on how to evaluate websites and on the IL framework.

Evaluation and testing

Evaluating process skills can be challenging as traditionally the academic curriculum rewards the product, and not specifically the process. The challenge for librarians is to turn skills into definable processes. Using the list specified in the KS3 strategy is a good starting point as it lists the competencies that information-literate students should have. The next step is to find methods of testing the pupil's abilities. The number, quality, and mix of the resources used can be ascertained from the inclusion of a bibliography. Resource evaluation sheets also reflect the student's ability to appraise different material. This process is simplified if the pupil is required to implement a set of rules or measurement criteria to their task.

Top Tip

> At the end of a series of lessons that focused on searching the Internet, the librarian gave the pupils a short, five-minute practical and theory test. The pupils were set the task of finding out the number of steps in the Eiffel tower and to write down how they did their search and to justify the final source that they choose. The outcome of the test was that the librarian learned that the pupils had a good grasp of keyword selection but were less able to justify their final website.

FAQs

The teacher complains that there is not enough time in the curriculum to teach IL skills

Introduce the idea of doing a starter or one lesson activity. Offer to help to prepare the materials and support the session. Ask one of your teacher-ambassadors to talk to this teacher.

One department complains that they have to do all the IL skills teaching

Use your evidence to demonstrate how the 'load' is being shared across the curriculum. Agree with the Head of Department as to the number of sessions to be included each year.

I can't get Department X interested

Set up a meeting with staff within the department to spot possible IL opportunities within the curriculum. If all else fails, then just move on. You can't win every battle. If the majority of subjects within the curriculum support the IL programme then, eventually, this department may wish to follow suit.

How do I get the message across?

Use departmental and INSET meetings to deliver your vision to staff and use your classroom experiences as examples of possible collaborations and pupil learning outcomes.

What are the benefits and drawbacks of integrated versus standalone sessions?

There are positives and negatives to both these approaches. You need to exploit every opportunity that you have. There seems to be a trend towards providing sixth-form students with a 'general studies' or 'wider studies' option. You could use this slot as an opportunity to teach students some general IL principles, but you must then communicate what you have taught these groups to other members of staff so that they know what they can expect from the pupils. Integrated sessions provide a context for the delivery of skills – you need to make sure that you negotiate with staff to ensure that there is the opportunity to discuss the skills that they need and that there is an opportunity to evaluate their progress.

Coffee and mints

Formulating an IL programme within a school is not an easy or quick process, but with determination and persuasion it is possible to deliver a vision of integrated IL skills within the curriculum. Spend your time wisely, and:

- get feedback from staff and pupils and review the sessions that you are providing;
- be flexible and offer to adapt and evolve sessions;
- communicate regularly with Senior Managers;
- work with subject staff to develop lessons;
- get the sessions written into the departmental handbook to ensure that they will run again the following year;
- join a professional group that can offer you support, ideas and guidance.

Finally, evaluate your progress and chart your achievements, use the tools that have been developed for school librarians to show the difference that you can make and ask other professionals for ideas as they may have the perfect 'recipe' for you to try.

Useful organisations

- SLA (School Library Association):*http://www.sla.org.uk/*
- SLG (School Libraries Group): *http://www.cilip.org.uk/specialinterestgroups/bysubject/school*
- SLN (School Librarians Network): to subscribe, e-mail: *sln-subscribe@yahoogroups.com* To read the archive, go to: *http://groups.yahoo.com/group/sln/messages*

Acknowledgements:

Contributions and examples of IL in action within schools were gratefully received from the following librarians: Helen Emery, Librarian and resources manager, King Edward IV School, Litchfield; Sue Blood, Librarian, Hurstpierpoint College, West Sussex; Sarah Pavey, College Librarian, Epsom College, Epsom; Fiona Dakers, Librarian, High School of Dundee, Dundee.

Notes

1. Since September 2006, MGC has merged with St James and the Abbey to become Malvern St James School.
2. Further analysis of different IL models can be found in Dubber (1999) and Herring (1999).
3. Strand 3, *How effective are teaching and learning*, is the most relevant part of this document for evaluating IL provision.
4. Not all schools run non-examined PSHE and Citizenship courses, but this may be an area that contains more flexibility than other academic courses.
5. A presentation that discusses the full set of games can be accessed from the LILAC   website (*http://www.cilip.org.uk/specialinterestgroups/bysubject/informationliteracy/lilac/lilac2006/parallels.htm*).
6. The school uses Moodle (*http://www.moodle.org*), a free software package.
7. Anne Robinson in her presentation entitled *'Making a difference'* at the SLG conference, York, April 2006.
8. CARS stands for Credibility, Accuracy, Reasonableness and Support.
9. Epsom College is a good example of a well-produced catalogue that has references to a range of materials and resource types

(*http://www.epsomcollege.org.uk/library.asp?menu=b*).

10. A presentation based on this project can be accessed from the LILAC 06 website (*http://www.cilip.org.uk/specialinterestgroups/bysubject/ informationliteracy/lilac/lilac2006/parallels.htm*).

References

Barrett, L. and Douglas, J. (2004) *The CILIP Guidelines for Secondary School Libraries,* 2nd edn. London: Facet.

Barrett, L. (2004) 'New guidelines, new challenges in schools', *Update*, 3(9): 30–1.

DfES (undated) '14–19 Gateway', available at *http://www.dfes.gov.uk/14-19/index.cfm?sid=1* (accessed 03 June 2006).

DfES (2001) 'Key stage 3 national strategy', available at *http://www.standards.dfes.gov.uk/keystage3/* (accessed 02 June 2006).

DfES (2004) *Improve Your Library: a Self-Evaluation Process for Secondary School Libraries and Learning Resource Centres*. London: DfES.

DfES (2004) *The School Library and the Key Stage 3 National Strategy Course Handbook*. London: DfES.

Dubber, G. (1999) *Developing Information Skills Through the Secondary School Library*. Swindon: SLA.

Eisenberg, M. and Berkowitz, B. (2001–2005) *The Big 6*. Available at *http://www.big6.com/* (accessed 15 June 2006).

Harris, R. (1997) 'Evaluating Internet research sources', available at *http://www.virtualsalt.com/evalu8it.htm* (accessed 20 June 2006).

Herring, J.E. (1999) *Exploiting the Internet as an Information Resource in Schools*. London: Library Association Publishing.

Jones, R. (2005) 'Information literacy and independent learning', *Update*, 4(1–2): 56.

Marland, M. (1984) *Information Skills in the Secondary Curriculum*. London: Methuen Educational.

Ofsted (2006) 'Good school libraries: making a difference to learning', available at *http://www.ofsted.gov.uk/publications/index.cfm?fuseaction=pubs .displayfile&id=4170&type=pdf* (accessed 23 March 2006).

Variety is the spice of life, or choosing your toppings with care: information literacy challenges in the further education sector

Gwyneth Price and Jane Del-Pizzo

The Further Education (FE) sector is the most diverse and complex area of education in the UK. The only realistic definition of its scope is that FE provides education for anyone over the compulsory school leaving age (16 years).

> FE colleges traditionally offered full- and part-time technical and vocational courses for students over compulsory school age (16) including adults, but have since broadened their role to offer programmes such as basic education courses, general education qualifications such as GCSEs and GCE A-levels, access to higher education programmes, tertiary level courses (under arrangement with external awarding bodies e.g. universities) and leisure courses for adults. Some colleges also provide vocational and work-related courses for 14- to 16-year-olds in partnership with schools Increasingly, courses leading to higher education qualifications, particularly those at sub-degree level such as the foundation degree are also provided in further education colleges. (Eurybase, 2007)

In practice, this means that FE students (over three million learners) will range in age from 14 to 80+, will be studying at levels ranging from vocational and non-award bearing (Level 1) to degree level and may be studying for anything from only an hour or two each week to full time.

'One of the sector's most striking features is its diversity and reach' (Foster, 2005). The learning that takes place within FE encompasses a range of formal and informal courses, vocational schemes and degree courses offered in conjunction with schools and higher education institutions.

The Department for Education and Skills (DfES) has recently released a White Paper entitled *Further education: raising skills, improving life chances* (DfES, 2006). The government strategy is to concentrate energies into the economic benefits of a skilled workforce, including providing opportunities for half of all young people to progress onto higher education. The Leitch review: *UK Skills: prosperity for all in the global economy – world class skills* published in December 2006 (Leitch, 2006) emphasises the need for the UK to become a leader in skills development. In January 2007 it was announced that compulsory education will be extended to the age of 18; all young people between the ages of 16 and 18 will be required to be engaged in education or training. The impact on the FE sector will depend very much on the level of funding agreed for this change, which is expected to take effect by 2013.

Information literacy (IL) skills are rarely recognised as essential to employability, and this is an area where FE librarians will need to prove their worth.

> Just look at the libraries in FE Colleges compared with those in HE; they are living proof of generations of under funding. (Coffield, 2006; 18)

The spread of courses from Level 1 to degree level presents a real challenge in tailoring your information sessions to your students' differing needs and learning styles. Students' previous experience of libraries is likely to be extremely varied, yet for many, libraries will open the doors to learning and opportunity. Flexibility is therefore the key to offering successful information sessions for these diverse groups, as is taking advantage of support from the variety of organisations that support skills training in further education subjects.

Information literacy education in FE and HE has many similarities but there is very little published exploration of the differences in needs of learners. CITSCAPES phase 2 website (*http://www.citscapes.ac.uk/*) provides a useful overview including considerations in relation to widening access and participation that are addressed through decentralisation and learning in a variety of work-based contexts; the move away from college-based study could prevent librarians providing appropriate and timely support. However college links with the local community and businesses could be further developed with library links.

The JISC (Joint Information Systems Committee) provides support for change in the use of ICTs and e-learning in FE colleges through its Regional Support Centres (RSCs). These RSCs are seen as 'a catalyst for change' (Pothen, 2006) and RSC staff provide practical assistance in developing resources within the e-learning environment. In practice, this means support for developing resources within Virtual Learning Environments (VLEs). These centres could also prove to be important in emphasising the relevance of information literacy to the e-learning agenda, and rolling out support and training.

A most important starting point for information literacy development at subject level is the Intute virtual training suite of tutorials (*http://www.vts.intute.ac.uk/*), covering topics in FE and HE and ranging from 'Agriculture, Food and Forestry' to 'Women's Studies' and from 'Health and Safety at Work' to 'Bioresearcher'. The tutorials have been developed by practising librarians and information specialists and are updated regularly. As there are built-in breaks within the tutorials, these can be chopped into manageable morsels to be digested over several short sessions and can be followed at each student's individual pace. There is a also a shopping basket of links that students can place websites of interest into – this has the advantage that it doesn't divert them from the tutorial but allows them to view all the websites they are interested in at the end of the session. Recent developments focus the need for evaluative skills when using Internet resources, and *The Internet Detective* has been relaunched with a strong emphasis on understanding plagiarism. This tutorial is an excellent starting place for many FE students, who may be new to using the Internet for research and see little wrong with the 'cut and paste' approach.

Planning for success

Essential to the success of any information literacy programme will be one or more confident and well-prepared teachers (or trainers) who have the full support of their managers and college tutors. If you don't already have a teaching qualification, you may want to consider attending a short, or more substantial course. What will help most is an understanding and empathy with learners in your institution, so find out as much as you can about the classes available and your students' backgrounds and experience. Understanding the basics of learning theory (see Chapter 8) and learning styles will boost your confidence and help you develop appropriate lesson plans.

There is evidence that people learn in different ways and a huge range of literature now focuses on the so-called Net generation (or Generation Y, the Google generation, etc). In reality not all FE students will fall into this category and there are still many young people who have not had the opportunity (or sometimes the inclination) to develop IT skills. Learning styles are not just about technology and its useful to consider how you learn best because that probably influences your teaching style too. The Inspiring Learning for All (ILFA) website offers information and tests to discover your learning style (*http://www.inspiringlearningforall.gov.uk/*), but its important to use these with a degree of scepticism (Coffield, 2004). In order to encourage our students to develop a range of learning strategies, and in order to support those who are unable to access certain kinds of material, it is helpful to consider different ways to present information and encourage learning.

When planning your menu it is vital to be aware of fundamental essential ingredients as well as the luxuries you might hope to include. If you are lucky enough to acquire asparagus, wild salmon or truffles its important to make the most of them. For much of the time, simple ingredients, simply presented will be sufficient as long as they appeal to your diners. In the words of chef Rick Stein:

> Keep the cooking simple and keep the ingredients good. (Stein, 1995)

Top Tip

Cook to your strengths. Every chef has a signature dish and they will try to include it in their standard menu; it will often be a challenging dish, but it's something they know they can do well and have the appropriate ingredients for to hand.

The menu

How often have you read a menu and felt none the wiser about what you will actually be eating? In the context of FE, it is important to sell your food. There are two key ways of getting people into a restaurant:

1. Provide a menu – this could be outside the door, on a website, on flyers; get reviewers to write about the food.
2. Let people taste the food.

We can do the same with our libraries. It's increasingly easy to produce publicity in a variety of ways but how easily can we get our potential users to 'taste' what is on offer?

Quick snacks

It is easy to forget that the staff who work at our information or enquiry desks are in fact offering quick information literacy snacks. Training for frontline staff should include an awareness of the ways in which students learn and how the right approach will encourage library users to want to learn more.

Special pizza menu

The complexities of providing an IL menu for the range of customers in FE suggests that simplicity really is the best policy. The pizza approach might be a good way to attract interest.

The pizza base

Think of the base as essentially a receptacle, though fortunately an edible one (thus saving waste and rubbish to be cleared at the end of the meal). Your pizza base will consist of generic information that all students and staff need to know; in general this is pretty factual – things like opening hours, how to access the website and catalogue, how materials are organised and so on. You might be able to afford to provide two thicknesses of pizza base (thick and thin) depending on the requirements of the group, or you might provide the thin base as standard with access to a thicker version via handouts, the VLE or website.

The toppings

These are of course the interesting part: you may decide to let the tutor decide for the whole group, or you might let students design their own pizza – and of course pizzas can have mixed toppings or be carefully divided into sections (rather like quattro formaggio). Your toppings can also be provided in a variety of formats. It will probably be standard to provide tomato and cheese – perhaps equating to basic search strategies and evaluation techniques as well as plagiarism awareness. Simple, easily obtainable, additions will be appropriate such as Intute tutorials and guides to using Google. For the more sophisticated palate you will provide help with using specific databases and electronic resources. Some guidance will be face-to-face demonstrations, some web- or VLE-based, others may be handouts, podcasts or make use of mobile technologies. And all of this can be eaten in the 'restaurant' (computer lab) or taken away. As Valentina Harris says:

> You cannot hurry a good thing. (Harris, 1998)

Doggie bags (pizza boxes) can be provided so no one feels they've got to eat everything there and then, but for those who want to stop and enjoy the experience you should provide a dessert – a special treat to enjoy at the end of the meal; something that your students will remember even if they forget some of the main course. Perhaps a demonstration of one or more of the JISC e-collections that you subscribe to, or something that relates to a particular assignment the students are working on. If there is time, ask for an evaluation of your session – perhaps a quick online form with the chance to win a prize, but you could equally provide this a week or so after the session and take the opportunity to remind students of ways in which the library or Learning Resources Centre (LRC) can provide further help.

Restaurant management

A successful meal is not solely dependant on the food, and never more so than when delivering to an FE audience. The fact of the matter is that the customer may not always be interested in eating and keeping them happy when for one reason or another they would rather be elsewhere is not always easy. Front of house staff in any business have to be prepared for unhappy customers and bad behaviour.

A few golden rules:

- Everyone is entitled to respect – and that includes you and your students.
- Always behave as if you expect the best from people, but be prepared for the worst. A sense of humour and interest in people are essential.
- Be flexible. If someone asks an interesting and relevant question, don't ignore or gloss over it, build it into your session. 'Inflexible planning

is the enemy of good eating' (David, 1998).

- Try to understand that there are good reasons why people may not be interested in what you have to offer, and try to think of ways to excite their appetite. Provide small tasty bites of interesting but not too strange offerings. Whatever you offer, make it as relevant as you possibly can – this is becoming easier now that tutors provide so much for their students online – if we can get access to course materials, we can judge the IL needs rather than relying on what the tutor feels we need to know.

The bottom line though is that you should never ignore interruptions – in an interactive classroom there should be time for questions and answers. If the interruption is disruptive, then you must stop talking and wait for silence and you should never be afraid to ask someone to leave. The important thing is to be confident in your approach to teaching and to find appropriate opportunities to improve your techniques; if you see yourself as a teacher and a person worthy of respect others will see you in the same light – you are a *chef*, not just a cook.

Taking risks

You will need to have some experience of working with large groups of students before you will be prepared to take risks with your teaching, but variety will certainly add to your pleasure and keep you fresh, particularly if you have numerous groups of new students to induct. An approach gaining in popularity is known as the 'Cephalonian method'; developed by Linda Davies and Nigel Morgan at Cardiff University and described by Nigel Morgan as 'a glorious fusion of colour, music and audience participation that is designed to appeal to the senses' (*http://www.infoteach.org/wiki/index.php/Cephalonian_method*). The method, based on a presentation at a holiday 'welcome' meeting, integrates the use of colour, music and humour to keep students focused; and of course there's no reason not to include food – unless your library rules forbid it! (Morgan and Davies, 2004)

Top Tip

Because of the diversity of students in FE, you will gain many ideas from the work of librarians in Schools and Higher Education; many, like the Cephalonian method, can be modified to suit different groups of learners.

Some specialist recipe ideas

Here follows a series of specialist recipes to inspire you while teaching. Don't be afraid to adapt these recipes to take account of local circumstances or tastes.

The amuse bouche

Ingredients:
PCs
Projector and screen
Interactive whiteboard
High staff to student ratio
Preparation time:
1–2 hours per week
Cooking time:
1–2 hours

Many further education institutions provide specialised courses for learning disabled students – these may include life skills, horticulture, car valeting or art classes. There is a challenge in providing sessions for learning disabled adults that reflect adult interests at a level that can be easily understood by a class that may have individuals with diverse capabilities. Communication with the tutor is key here (see the dim sum recipe below). A recent article by Williams et al. (2006) suggests that there are many perceived benefits of using information and communications technology with students with special educational needs

Repetition and building slowly on achievements will yield results as well as inspiring confidence in learning disabled adults. For some students, mastering mouse skills such as double-clicking will be a real achievement. A very good place to start with is Peepo's website (*http://www.peepo.com/*), which displays a version of the BBC webpage suitable for people with learning disabilities who may find using a mouse difficult. All the icons on the site are large, which helps students with dexterity problems and the pages looks uncluttered, taking out some of the visual disturbance that can prove confusing on some webpages.

Using an interactive whiteboard within a small group, encourage students to volunteer to click backwards and forwards between webpages to find images or words, with plenty of encouragement given for all attempts. Depending on the subject the students are studying, identifying and marking pictures on a whiteboard can improve recall of subject matter, coordination and confidence in using ICT. Williams et al. (2006) give the example of a task of identifying hazards in a kitchen: the literature suggests that using a virtual kitchen is as effective as using a real life example.

Dim sum

Ingredients:
Plenty of patience and energy!
As many staff to students as you feel you need
Computer and table areas set aside for the session
Flipchart
Assignment title(s)
Photocopies of book indexes
Photocopies of tables of contents from journals
Catalogue searches
Web searches
Short evaluation sheets – these shouldn't take more than a moment to fill out.
Preparation time:
2 hours approx
Discussion with the tutor/lecturer
Photocopying and question setting
Cooking time:
1–2 hours

The just-in-time approach is effective in working in concert with the tutor's timetable in preparing their students for their first major assignment. At that point, the students are more likely to be focusing on the skills and information they need to acquire to complete any assignment with a research element. Agreeing with the tutor the outcomes of the session is key to success: if they convey a negative approach to the session it is unlikely to be successful with the students. Talk to the tutor of the group and ascertain which are the key concepts the question(s) are trying to examine. Are there any particular concepts that the students need to focus on? This will be important in guiding the first part of the session. What is the group like? Are they self-confident? Is asking for contributions within a large group situation appropriate? Make sure that the tutor can also attend the session and will work with you to achieve the outcomes of the session. Good communication with tutors is key to successfully impacting on students' approach to information seeking and handling. If possible run sessions for teaching staff before approaching them to do the same for students. There will usually be a split between those staff who are aware of the plethora of supporting websites, subject gateways and the importance of teaching students how to handle and incorporate information into their work, and those who are not. The aim should be to champion this knowledge, whether it's within a formal training session to staff, quick informal demo, or spreading the word within faculty/team meetings.

Within the first few minutes of the group arriving, get them brainstorming keywords based on the assignment titles that both you and they have been given. Given your prior discussion with the tutor, this can be undertaken either in a large group or by breaking the students up into smaller groups.

Teenage groups can often benefit from dim sum or a moveable feast. Split your group into three or four smaller groups and get them working in groups on an activity. This could include searching photocopies of a book index to get them locating the keywords they've previously specified and using synonyms and antonyms. Another group could be engaged in employing the same techniques to search the online catalogue to raise awareness of locating library resources. Students can also be guided to using basic search techniques within any appropriate online databases. These first sessions are also a good opportunity to steer students away from Google, for the time being at least, and an opportunity to introduce students to subject gateways. There are a number of options you can employ for this – the takeaway option is Intute tutorials, however it is possible to build your own list of trusted sites and to enable students to search through them through the use of Rollyo (*http://www.rollyo.com/*).

Remember to give feedback forms to students at the end of sessions – this provides useful statistics on the worth of the sessions and how they can be refined for future use.

Soup and a sandwich

Ingredients:
PCs with access to the Internet
Projector and screen/interactive whiteboard (if available)
Weblinks illustrating the dangers of the free web

Cooking time:
15–20 minutes

Sandwiching sessions between classes, can help students to find their way through a soup of information! The reality is that despite educators' best efforts, many students will still visit Google to conduct at least some of their research. There are plenty of ways to help them search more effectively and a lunchtime or evening session can be promoted in terms of delivering time-saving benefits to students who attend.

The sessions can also be used to highlight the drawbacks of searching the free web and draw attention to forthcoming information sessions on other resources. Use some preselected websites to illustrate that, although a website may contain all the keywords and may rank highly on Google, it might not necessarily be a trusted source.

Although some of Google's recent endeavours have caused some controversy with regard to their copyright and intellectual property implications, it would be worth exploring Google Scholar, Google Books and the Librarian Center to see whether they could deliver benefits to your students.

Perhaps a final practical task we might suggest is to ask students to identify the most useful websites with information about healthy eating – with the help of Google and Intute – and provide some healthy snacks to eat during the session.

Conclusions

Working in the FE sector is always going to be challenging due to the diversity of learners and the differing levels of engagement and interest they have in their subject. However, it is also a hugely rewarding sector for librarians to work in, and one where information literacy teaching can really make a big impact on people's lives and their future ability to become a lifelong learner. There are many synergies and interrelated concerns in the education sector as a whole and information literacy is an issue that we should be tackling strategically. While it is important to network with others in the FE sector, collaboration with librarians in both schools and HE is essential if we want to really make progress

References

Coffield, F. (2004) 'Should we be using learning styles? what research has to say to practice', *Learning and Skills Research Centre*, available at *https://www.lsneducation.org.uk/* (accessed 29 January 2007).

Coffield, F. (2006) 'Running ever faster down the wrong road: an alternative future for education and skills', available at *http://www.ioe.ac.uk/schools/leid/lss/FCInauguralLectureDec06.doc* (accessed 29 January 2007).

David, E. (1998) 'French provincial cooking', quoted in J. Norman (ed). *South Wind Through the Kitchen: the Best of Elizabeth David*. Harmondsworth: Penguin; p.14.

DfES (2006) *Further Education: Raising Skills, Improving Life Chances*. Available at *http://www.dfes.gov.uk/publications/furthereducation/* (accessed 8 March 2007).

Eurybase (2007) *The Education System in the United Kingdom (England, Wales and Northern Ireland)*. Available at *http://194.78.211.243/Eurybase /Application/frameset.asp?country=UK&language=VO* (accessed 2 January 2007).

Foster, A. (2005) *Realising the Potential: a Review of the Future Role of Further Education Colleges*. London: DfES. Available at *http://www.dfes.gov.uk /furthereducation/uploads/documents/REALISING06.pdf* (accessed 29 January 2007).

Gardner, K. (2007) 'Breaking the mould: the study centre approach', *Library and Information Update*, 6(1–2): 36–9.

Harris V. (1998) *Risotto! Risotto!* London: Cassell; p. 8.

Leitch, S. (2006) *Prosperity for All in the Global Economy: World Class Skills: Final Report*. London: The Stationery Office. Available at *http://www.hm-treasury.gov.uk/media/523/43/leitch_finalreport051206.pdf* (accessed 8 March 2007).

Morgan, N. and Davies, L. (2004) 'Innovative library induction – introducing the 'Cephalonian Method'' *Sconul Focus*, 32(2). Available at *https://www.sconul.ac.uk/publications/newsletter/32/2.pdf* (accessed 8 March 2007).

Pothen, P. (2006) 'A catalyst for change'. *JISC Inform*, 15. Available at *http://www.jisc.ac.uk/media/documents/publications/inform%2015-final.pdf* (accessed 8 March 2007).

Stein, R. (1995). *Rick Stein's Taste of the Sea*. London: BBC Books; p.12.

Williams, P., Jamali, H.R. and Nicholas, D. (2006) 'Using ICT with people with special education needs: what the literature tells us', *Aslib Proceedings*, 58(4), 330–45.

8

Information literacy beef bourguignon (also known as information skills stew or i-skills casserole): the higher education sector

Jane Secker, Debbi Boden and Gwyneth Price

This is a favourite among those carefully composed, slowly cooked dishes....Such dishes do not, of course, have a rigid formula, each cook interpreting it according to her taste. Elizabeth David on Boeuf a la Bourguignonne (Norman, 1998; p. 122).

Laying the table

The concept of information literacy (IL) is probably more developed among the library profession in higher education (HE) than in other sectors. Arguably, the role of the librarian as a teacher is more firmly established and most academic libraries have had some form of training programme in place for at least a decade. In part this has been driven by technology and the availability of high-speed network connections and electronic resources. But it is also part of the wider recognition in higher education in particular, of the central role of the library (and the librarian) in learning support. This chapter largely draws on the experiences of the authors in the higher education sector in the UK, but the importance of information literacy is widely recognised in higher education throughout the world. In fact, until recently, in North America, Australasia and parts of Scandinavia the concept and importance of information literacy was much more established than in the UK.

There have been several changes in HE over the last decade that arguably have led to an increased recognition for the need for information literacy and for library staff to become more actively engaged in teaching. The Follett Report (Joint Funding Council's Libraries Review Group, 1993), the eLib programe (JISC, 2006; Rusbridge, 1998) – notably EduLib (JISC, 1998), as well as continuing developments in new technology have been catalysts for change, not least the ubiquity of technology, from mobile phones to laptops, that permeates all aspects of society. In the UK today e-learning is a reality for many students, with almost all HE institutions now using a virtual learning environment (VLE) or engaging in some form of e-learning. Secker (2004) provides a detailed account of e-learning and its impact on the role of librarians. The enormous growth in electronic resources available in academic libraries has also hastened the need to provide an increasing variety of detailed library induction programmes and training classes. Students frequently need to grapple with multiple passwords and interfaces to access resources and use the multitude of library databases now available. These tools are often a sharp contrast to the habits of the 'Google generation' that use one simple search box and believe it finds everything. Information literacy is an important weapon to challenge those who fail to see the continuing relevance of libraries. The developments in Web 2.0 and social software are providing new tools and challenges for librarians to work alongside students.

In the UK, the 'widening participation' agenda and the enormous growth in the numbers of students entering higher education – from increasingly diverse backgrounds – has also led to a greater need for information literacy courses. Gone are the days when a typical undergraduate student comes fresh out of school at 18 and studies full time, living on the university campus. Students today can increasingly be mature, part-time and/or studying at a distance from the institution. They may have part-time jobs, children or other dependants and their motivations for entering higher education are increasingly diverse.

Universities themselves have also changed significantly, growing in terms of the number of institutions and the range of subjects they teach. In the UK the most notable distinction is between the older, traditional research-led institutions, and new post-1992 universities that focus more on teaching and tend to offer more diverse vocational subjects. HE typically provides teaching to students from Foundation level to postgraduate degrees, with a growing emphasis on the needs of Doctoral students and developments within continuing professional development for the professions. A useful overview of the UK HE sector is provided by Brophy, in Levy and Roberts (2005). However, these differences mean that generalising about practice within the sector can be misleading. Moreover, conceptions of IL and of the role of librarians do differ. The HE sector in the UK and throughout the world is therefore extremely diverse, and it embraces a range of institutions of differing sizes, ages and with significantly diverse intakes of students. All this means that in one chapter we can really only scratch the surface and provide basic ideas about how to teach information literacy. Therefore, rather than assemble a meal, we have tried to give ideas of flavours and ingredients that work well together. Teaching in HE can be likened in many ways to preparing tapas. You may need numerous small dishes that can be served up in a variety of combinations that are adaptable and that cater for a huge variety of tastes and preferences. Dishes may stand alone, or be served up to form a whole meal. Dishes may be delivered in a formal classroom setting or virtually, via online support. Flexibility is often the key to success, but it is also important to tap into academic concerns and wherever possible collaborate with teaching staff.

Whetting the appetite: appetisers and nibbles

In the HE sector, engaging with senior managers and with academic staff is one of the most important things librarians can do. It is therefore essential to have a clear definition of information literacy both as a concept, but also as a set of standards that students can be measured against. Non-library staff may be unfamiliar with the term information literacy so having to hand a useful brief definition is essential. The Chartered Institute of Library and Information Professionals (CILIP) have defined IL as: '...knowing when and why you need information, where to find it, and how to evaluate, use and communicate it in an ethical manner' (CILIP, 2006). Most academic staff can relate to this concept, particular when one uses practical examples such as 'it's about finding quality sources' or 'learning how to reference properly'. There are many other definitions available from organisations such as the American Library Association (ALA), the Council of Australian University Librarians (CAUL), and as recently as 2005 JISC introduced the concept of 'i-skills' (JISC, 2005). Other publications include Christine Bruce's *Seven Faces of Information Literacy* (Bruce, 1997) and Michael Eisenberg and Robert Berkowitz *Big Six Skills* (Eisenberg and Berkowitz, 2007). However, the remit for those involved in the creation of the CILIP definition was to produce a definition in simple language that could be adapted as required depending on the audience. The definition provides a good basis for HE and the ethical element immediately engages staff who are often increasingly concerned with plagiarism.

The aim of any IL course is to develop the IL skills of the users, and the CILIP definition provides us with a starting point, as this is what we want to achieve. Competencies however, are then required to measure what skills are needed to create the information-literate student or academic. In 1999, the Information Skills Task Force, on behalf of SCONUL (Society of College, National and University Libraries), prepared a positioning paper on IL skills in the HE sector (SCONUL,1999). From this paper emerged the SCONUL Seven Pillars model (Figure 8.1; SCONUL, 2006). The Seven Pillars have become a standard that many within HE use when developing IL courses. CILIP have also developed a set of competencies that can be used in conjunction with the Seven Pillars.

Figure 8.1   The SCONUL Seven Pillars

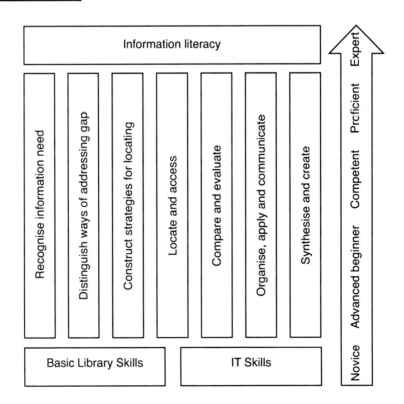

A great deal of literature is available on the subject of IL. Bruce and Lampson's research, completed in 2001, noted that a search on the Internet using the keywords 'information literacy' 'retrieved between 5,700 and 9,500 items' (Bruce and Lampson, 2002). In January 2007 a Google phrase search retrieved 1,060,000 items! Judging from the number of UK conferences and seminars based on IL, we know it is a subject open to much debate within the country. Engaging academic staff with information literacy as a concept may mean introducing them to the published literature. It may also help if we as librarians are actively involved in the research community, through presenting at conferences and publishing articles. Therefore, underpinning any student information literacy programme in higher education should be a staff development programme that not only focuses on up-skilling academic and administrative staff, but ensures they recognise the importance of IL as a wider concept.

However, engaging academic staff and senior managers in our own institutions is only the first stage, as the importance of IL needs to be recognised by central government in the UK. In 1996, The Dearing Report recommended the introduction of Key Skills into post-16 education. If at this point one of the key skills being recommended had been IL, we may have seen a different scenario. As Sheila Corrall has remarked, 'the UK government is committed to electronic delivery of information but has yet to recognise the need for an information-literate population to make e-government a meaningful concept' (Buckley Owen, 2003). In the US, IL is being driven from the top down, yet in the UK it is very much being driven from the bottom up. Librarians in the UK, however, have not been resting on their laurels and research 'revealed many instances of good practice within institutions' (thebigblue, 2003). Organisations such as JISC (Joint Information Systems Committee) and the Arts and Humanities Research Board (AHRB) are providing grants for research into IL and we are reaping the benefits with projects such as thebigblue, the GAELS project, JUBILLEE and Webber and Johnston's study into 'UK academics' conceptions of, and pedagogy for, information literacy'. All these projects had different agendas but they provide an valuable insight into the student and academics perception of IL, collaboration between faculty and the library, evolutionary differences in e learning between disciplines, assessment and current practice in IL training in HE. Recent initiatives include Eduserv sponsoring the development of the cross-sectoral IL website and providing funding for IL research projects.

Preparing the chef: the need for staff development

IL has become a core part of many librarians' roles within the HE sector, although it seems there is reluctance by some within the sector to recognise this. Bruce and Lampson suggest a reticence by some professionals at having to break away from tradition and 'impose an evaluation opinion on sources' and also having to teach critical evaluation and analysis (Bruce and Lampson, 2002). Part of the reticence may come from a lack of confidence in teaching skills and pedagogic understanding. While Library Schools are beginning to recognise the importance of IL, there is little within their curriculum that prepares LIS students with both the practicalities and theory of teaching. New graduates often discover that they require a set of new skills starting with a basic understanding of IL and knowledge of pedagogy, including terminology such as learning objectives, learning styles, course design and assessment. They may also need to have the skill to manage group behaviour, to develop online courses using VLEs, to collaborate with academics, IT specialists and learning technologists. While changes is slow to filter through from library schools, this need is currently being met through continuing professional development events and through attendance at conferences such as the Librarians Information Literacy Annual Conference (LILAC).

The chef's repertoire

Whatever the chef's training and experience there are certain skills and understanding that will be essential for success. For the teaching (or training) librarian, these are likely to include and understanding of how learning takes place and an appropriate level of confidence in classroom management.

What is learning?

Learning is the process of active engagement with experience. It is what people do when they want to make sense of the world. It may involve the development or deepening of skills, knowledge, understanding, awareness, values, ideas and feelings, or an increase in the capacity to reflect. Effective learning leads to change, development and the desire to learn more. (MLA, 2004)

Taking some time to think about learning is a useful experience for all library staff and an enjoyable opportunity for staff training. The MLA's *Inspiring Learning for All* website (MLA, 2004) provides excellent material to support this. For staff engaged in teaching HE students, reflection on their own learning experiences can lead to a much greater understanding of how to support others.

Pedagogic knowledge is important when planning a course and having a good understanding of learning theories will make planning and developing your course mush easier. It also ensures that your dinner is of good quality and that you are not confusing techniques such as folding and whipping! No one is saying that only trained chefs can cook, similarly it is not necessary for most librarians to become a qualified teacher. Nevertheless, understanding some of the theories of learning will help even the most experienced librarian.

- If you are working with academics that are committed to their students, they will use an understanding of how students learn to enhance their teaching. If you want to be seen as a teacher, rather than a presenter, you will need to understand the language of teaching.

- If you feel uncomfortable with teaching large groups and feel that you are not getting through to the students, it may be that a better understanding of how they learn may help.

- Preparing a teaching session for a group of students who you have never met and know nothing about is rather like preparing a meal for a large group of strangers – if you don't know their tastes, fads and appetites, you may have to play very safe or risk leaving some of them to go hungry.

Learning theories

There is no shortage of material to read and an increasing number of excellent courses of varying lengths. There are some very specific issues for librarians so it is worth going on a specialist course if you can find one. *Teaching Information Skills* by Webb and Powis (2004) provides an excellent overview of learning theories, as does Philippa Levy's chapter in Levy and Roberts (2005). For a more challenging discussion of learning theory in an electronic environment, see Conole and Oliver (2007). Here is a basic overview of some learning theories: including Behaviourism, cognitivism, social learning theories and experimental learning.

Behaviourism

Pavlov was a proponent of behaviourism and his experiments with dogs to persuade them to salivate when a bell rang – even when food wasn't forthcoming – are well known. Behaviourist theories indicate that you can change behaviour without changing attitudes and beliefs; not at all what we're trying to achieve with information literacy but of course we may find that sanctions will persuade students to turn off their mobile phones even when all else fails!

Cognitivism

Cognitivist theorists include Piaget and Vygotsky, and their theories recognise that learners need to progress through a series of stages. There are few people who can create a three-course gourmet meal from a recipe book without any previous experience of cooking and equally few students who can search a bibliographic database without appropriate skills and understanding. Cognitivist theories suggest that development can only be extended through intervention and the provision of 'scaffolding', learning will be incremental, building on stages and moving to the 'zone of proximal development'. There is not much room here for the sudden leap of understanding, the appreciation of food and how flavours and textures work together that help a cook create a brilliant meal without formal training. Library skills teaching will benefit from a 'scaffolding' approach, an understanding of the stages a student will need to go through before becoming information competent.

Social learning theories

Social learning theories recognise the role of social issues, such as gender, peer group, class and race on learning, as well as environmental issues. If we can afford fine ingredients and the best tools for the job as well as a state of the art kitchen, it may be easier to turn out good meals. Students who come to Higher Education without experience of well-funded libraries may be at a disadvantage and of course peer group pressures may affect willingness to spend time in a library or a kitchen.

Experiential learning

Kolb's well-known theory (Figure 8.2) focuses on experience as the key to learning. A serious cook will focus on tastes and flavours and think how to recreate and improve on them in their own kitchen. The experience of cooking and eating leads to experimentation, tasting and refining of the recipe. Similarly there is a connection between a desire to learn and the development of information literacy; we are fortunate that twenty-first century students have access to the tools so they can refine and practice search techniques rather than depending on the intervention of a librarian.

Figure 8.2 Kolb's theory of learning

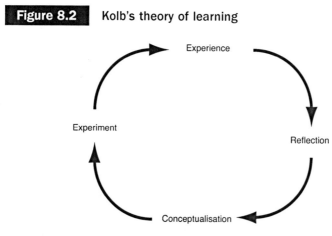

Constructivism

Constructivism recognises that learning is not a passive activity; it is affected by a whole mix of issues, including environment, experience and personality. This means that a teaching session that works with one group of students may not work with another for all sorts of reasons that we may or may not be able to influence. Just as the freshness of ingredients, the size of an egg or the oven temperature may affect the outcome when using a standard recipe, the success of the meal will also be affected by the individual tastes, appetite or mood of those eating. As teachers we have to focus on strategies for dealing with the variety of outcomes and doing our best to enhance the learning experience

Situated learning and communities of practice

The work of Lave and Wenger is heavily influential in HE and emphasises the need for participants to feel part of a learning community or a community of practice, to feel at home within their academic field and accepted by their peers. Just as when we cook, we feel flattered if a friend compliments our cooking but we would only feel really confident of our abilities if invited to work with a well-known chef; acceptance into their community of practice is a most important driver for any ambitious postgraduate or doctoral student.

Learning styles

It is important to recognise that people learn in different ways and have preferences about how they learn. In addition, provision of learning materials in a variety of formats will help disabled students feel active members of the class. For more on learning styles and research into learning style analyses, see Chapter 7.

Classroom management

Teaching large groups of undergraduates with preconceived ideas about libraries is not always easy, so it is best to prepare yourself in two ways:

1. Be clear about what you consider to be inappropriate behaviour and be prepared to deal with it. If you don't know what is considered rudeness in the context in which you work it is best to talk to colleagues both in and outside the library.
2. Pre-empt difficult behaviour by making sessions as interactive and enjoyable as possible. Information literacy is not a dull topic!

Top Tips when teaching

We all have different styles of teaching but here are a few tips that may help you:

- Make sure you can see a clock easily. If there isn't a wall clock, take off your watch and keep that visible so you know what the time is.
- Hand out a register for everyone to sign. As some students' handwriting can be illegible it is even better if you can get the names beforehand and print out a register so that they can put their signature next to their name! The register means you can easily keep a record of the number of people who have attended.
- Before you begin the session, introduce yourself (and anyone else who is helping with the session), and name the course and the department and/or year you are teaching. This ensures you have the right group of students.

Top Tip continued

- Do make eye contact and smile.

- Ask everyone to ensure that their mobile phones are either turned off or on 'silent'.

- Ask everyone to refrain from using their computers during the presentation: a good phrase is 'it can be offputting for everyone to hear a keyboard tapping away in the background'. And you can mention how irritating you find it! Do not be afraid to ask someone to stop 'tapping' if they 'forget' that you have asked them not to.

- You can ask people to turn off their monitors. This takes away the temptation for people to tap on their keyboards!

- Ask everyone to stop talking during the presentation, but emphasise that talking during hands-on sessions is fine – it often helps people learn.

- Briefly explain the structure of the session, so that the students will know what to expect when.

- If you have 'break-out' sessions, tell the students how long they have for the task/discussion/etc.

- When you have finished the session, allow 5 minutes before it is timetabled to end for the evaluation sheets to be handed out and completed.

Adapted from: *iLIP – Internal Information Literacy Programme* (Imperial College London, 2005).

The event: from canapés and snacks to a four course banquet

Information literacy 'events' in higher education, like cooking, can take a wide variety of forms, for example your institution may recognise the value of 'library training' or it may be seen as a one-off activity that takes place as part of induction. The start of the year and the intake of new students is a key time to run training events that may be part of a regular cycle of generic training offered by the library or may be specific induction events following requests from academic staff. If induction activities or short sessions are all you are currently being offered by staff then view these as IL snacks or canapés, which hopefully will show off your abilities in the kitchen and lead to commissions for four course banquets in the future! Increasingly, IL is seen as a key skill and some institutions have taken a strategic approach to ensuring their students are information literate by running specific programmes of training, which may be generic or tailored to specific subjects. In other institutions the value of IL may be less widely recognised and it may involve being opportunistic as staff request one-off sessions at specific times of year, e.g. the start of the dissertation 'season' often leads to a request for one-off sessions on literature searching or citing and referencing. Before you start planning your 'event' or menu, flexibility is really the key – and being explicit about what topics you can cover and how long it will realistically take. Staying with the menu approach, McConnell Library at Radford University in the States offers an 'a la carte' menu of IL training that academic staff are invited to pick and choose from. Staff can see at a glance the range of topics on offer and the length of time a typical session will take (for more information see *http://lib.radford.edu/Instruction/menu.asp*).

Preparation

The success of any recipe depends very much on the preparation, be it a small simple dish or a complex gourmet meal. If you have prepared properly you will feel confident about the quality of your dish and its final presentation. Part of your preparation includes how you market your programme to the academic departments. It can sometimes difficult to know whether to try market IL as a concept before you develop your programme or whether you should have the programme completed and ready to demonstrate before you try and market it. The most practical way is to have a plan of your programme and one developed unit to show to academic staff. Try developing the unit that they will recognise as the most useful to them. For example, a unit on plagiarism or referencing is usually a good one to demonstrate.

Liaison with academic departments

Liaison with academic departments is a very important part of your preparation. There are many different scenarios; here are some examples:

1. You have been asked to create a course by the academic department – liaison is therefore much easier. You need however to try to ensure the following:

- enough time in the student timetable, preferably staggered and timetabled so you are teaching students at a time of need;
- that the course is linked to an academic module and has subject relevance – teaching students how to find appropriate resources when they have just received their first assignment helps put what you are teaching in context;
- that the sessions are compulsory and, if possible, credit-bearing;
- that you have proper evaluation and feedback mechanisms so you can demonstrate the worth of what you are doing and how it makes a difference.

2. You already have timetabled sessions but they are in a lecture format and you want to develop a more active learning approach and use PCs for hands-on sessions. You will need to:

- approach the department early before they start timetabling for the next year as you will be asking for more timetabled hours – the increase may be considerable if you have large numbers and only have access to small PC labs;
- plan your campaign – you must think through carefully what you are going to say and explain to the department how changing the way you teach will benefit the students and them;
- use library-friendly academics to help put your case forward, ask them to drop into conversation with appropriate colleagues that you are creating a new and exciting interactive programme that will really benefit the students;
- try to approach the person in the department who has overall responsibility for the degree programme;
- take along example of what you intend to do and stress the benefits for each section of the programme;
- ensure you have proper evaluation and feedback mechanisms so you can demonstrate the worth of what you are doing and how it makes a difference.

3. You have no timetabled sessions:
- Don't aim too high to start with. A pilot of your programme is usually the best way forward. This way you are not setting yourself up to fail and a pilot allows you to iron out problems before you try launching the programme to the other departments.

- Remember that academics are often not unsympathetic to what you are trying to achieve, but timetabling is often tight so you have to make a really good case as to why they should find time.

- Plan your campaign. Sound out a few friendly academics, sell the benefits of the programme. Gain their support and if possible find some one to agree to pilot your new programme. Then approach the person in the department who has overall responsibility of for the degree programme.

- If you are planning to develop an online programme find examples that you can demonstrate or take along your one created unit; explain the benefits to them and their students. If you are in a new university, it may be useful to talk about retention; in an old university, plagiarism may be a more appropriate topic.

- Ensure you have proper evaluation and feedback mechanisms so you can demonstrate the worth of what you are doing and how it makes a difference.

Planning your meal

If you are planning a special meal and have total control over all aspects of the venue, date and time, menu and guests and the costs, you can start from scratch and create the perfect event; the same might be true of planning a learning event. In theory you should plan in the 'right' order and experts suggest that this is the order in which it should be completed:

1. specify aims and learning outcomes;

2. plan how to check that learning outcomes have been attained, i.e. assessment;

3. plan the learning activities;

4. plan the inputs, e.g. presentation, handouts, activities – ingredients and store cupboard;

5. sequence and timetable the session;

6. decide on the appropriate learning environment or delivery method;

7. plan how to get feedback.

In practice there will be certain aspects of the situation over which you have little or no control:

- the course tutor may have preconceived ideas of the content;
- the date and time may already be fixed;
- you have to use whatever rooms are available, or there may be an expectation that you will use the VLE;
- the group size is predetermined;
- the staff available may have only limited teaching expertise.

Much of this may be negotiable, but your planning will have to be pragmatic and may often be more like brainstorming and lateral thinking; mind-mapping tools can be helpful for planning an event as well as in your teaching. However you go about it, it really is worthwhile to produce a lesson plan (Appendix 8.1) as it particularly helps to avoid the lazy cooks method of adding whatever comes to hand. Nevertheless, any plan should be flexible enough to allow for questions and student involvement.

Planning a banquet

If you are planning a major teaching event or a series of sessions, you would do well to use project planning techniques to avoid disaster:

- if your menu requires cross team working or input from other departments, make sure everyone is kept informed during the planning stage;
- confirm who will be head chef;
- prepare a project initiation document (PID), and ensure everyone agrees to the menu and the time scales involved;
- hold regular meetings to ensure there are no problems;
- use the traffic light system:
  green – everything is on track;
  amber – some of the ingredients are near their sell by date;
  red – the ingredients are mouldy and the shops are shut!

Top Tip

If you are not used to managing projects, check out the staff development programme at your institution; they may have courses that can help you. Useful hints on project management can be found at *http://www.mindtools.com/pages/main/newMN_PPM.htm*

The learning environment

You would normally start planning for your guests by creating your menu and gathering your ingredients; however, it may be sensible to consider how you are going to deliver and present your meal first; whether you intend to offer silver service (face-to-face) or self-service (online). Although you may not have any choice over delivery as you may not have access to a VLE or webpages, if you do this needs to be considered before you start planning your menu. This is simply because planning your menu will depend on the type of delivery you choose.

If you have the ability to provide online delivery, you need to consider the following before deciding whether it is the most appropriate delivery mechanism.

- Benefits of online programmes:
    - they can be accessed anytime, any place where there is Internet access (this is particularly beneficial for distance learners, students who are on placement or part-time students);
    - they act as a reference tool and learning resource for all students;
    - students can learn at their own pace at a point of need;
    - they are helpful for students whose first language is not English;
    - they may be helpful for disabled students;
    - they can provide useful management information.

- Disadvantages of online programmes:
    - they do not match everyone's learning style;
    - students need appropriate IT skills;
    - students need access to the Internet and a PC off campus;
    - materials need to be in a format that will speedily load with a dial-up connection;
    - access can cost students money if they are using a dial-up connection;
    - they increase printing costs.

- Other things to think about:
    - Will your materials be generic or subject specific?
    - How can you ensure the programme will be sustainable?
    - Who manages the programme?
    - Who ensures the programme is kept up to date (this includes content and the physical up loading of content in your online programme)?
    - What are your quality assurance procedures?
    - Do you have a strategic plan for the future of IL development?
    - Are you taking a web-focused or a blended learning approach?

Ingredients and store cupboard

Before preparing for your meal, it is always wise to check what you have in your store cupboard as this will affect your menu. If you have little or no budget your store cupboard may be all you have to work with, but if you have a budget it will inform on the ingredients you need to buy. There are two main ingredients that you should always try to have when cooking; the goodwill of your senior management team and a good understanding of the staff and academic programmes you are supporting. Without these, your soufflé may sink! Try to ensure that the benefits to your users are clear and understood by the academics and the senior management of the library. More importantly, make sure that what you are doing supports the library strategic plan.

The quality of ingredients that you use is important, but sometimes you can't afford to buy organic or you just don't have time to go shopping and you have to use what is in the cupboard. Try to remember to keep your store cupboard well stocked, and throw away any items that have passed their sell by date. Obvious ingredients may for example include:

- teaching materials (evaluation forms, presentations, lesson plans etc) and courses already written;
- software available e.g. online assessment software such as Question Mark Perception or the Informs tutorials;
- library catalogue documentation and help guides;
- databases and e-journal documentation and help guides;
- equipment including: laptop, projector, extension cable, extended network cable, memory sticks, acetates, writable CDs.

Sometimes you may not always know what is in the cupboard, as things may have been put there by other chefs. You may have to look hard to find these things as they may not be obvious, for example:

- If you are planning an online course will it be on the institutional website or does the institution have a VLE?
- If you intend to use the institutional website, does it have a content management system?
- Is there an institutional Web Master who will be able to help you develop your ideas?
- If you intend to use a VLE, does the institution have more than one?

- Find out who else is using a VLE for teaching; have they purchased specialist software?

- Would the software be suitable for your needs, and if so does it have a site license? (Don't fall into the trap of using technology for the sake of it!)

- Do you have appropriate pedagogic knowledge – which of the library staff are trained teachers?

- What support is available from your teaching and learning department/s?

Top Tip

Create a resource check list (Table 8.1). This is a really helpful way of creating a quick overview of your resources and of ones you will need to acquire.

Table 8.1   Example of part of a resource list for a project to develop an online IL course

Resource check list								
Resource	Yes	No	Action	Location	Internal	External	Cost (£)	Notes
VLE	Y			Store cupboard	Y		0	University VLE
Library staff who have used VLE before		Y	University in house training	University teaching and learning staff	Y		0	
Pedagogic knowledge – course design		Y	External training course	London		yes	280 plus travel	
Content	Y	Y		Store cupboard and library staff	Y		0	Some content available but new content will require writing
Staff with Power Point knowledge	Y			Library	Y		0	

Methods

Learning activities

There are many approaches and combinations you can choose from when delivering your meal. Blended learning approaches are often popular with students (Boden and Holloway, 2004; 35). Blended learning allows you to use a combination of delivery methods in both formal and informal settings. Table 8.2 shows just a few things you can combine when using the blended learning approach.

Table 8.2 The blended approach

Face-to-face demonstration	Online learning units using VLE or a web-based course
Face-to-face lecture	Workshops
Hands-on with worksheets	Different media – video, DVD, personal response systems etc.
Hands-on with online tutorials	Communication using e-mail, chat, blogs, online discussions, mobile technologies
Wikis	Drop-in and timetabled surgeries

Assessment

'The proof of the pudding is in the eating.' (Fourteenth century English proverb)

Assessment is an essential part of any course. You know what the learning outcomes, aims and objectives you have for the students, but how do you know they have reached the level of learning they require? Different types of assessment may include:

- Formative assessment is an informal way of a student or tutor assessing learning. This type of assessment is not marked, but may subsequently be submitted for summative assessment.

- Summative assessment is a formal type of assessment that a student submits for marking, a typical example in an IL programme would be a quiz (online or paper). This type of assessment allows you to quickly assess if a student is having problems and in need of further instruction.

- questionnaire allows you to see the level of understanding a student has at the beginning of a course. The post-course questionnaire demonstrates the level of learning achieved by the end of the course.

- Personal response systems (PRS) – allow you to ask students questions in a more interactive and fun way. Answers are recorded and can be analysed immediately. These can be used anonymously either in group work or individually, or individuals allocated a specific handset so their work can be monitored.

- Critical analysis sheet – a critical analysis sheet can be used if a student has completed an assignment for the academic department. Students are asked to consider the search strategy they used for their assignment. They are then expected to draw on the skills and concepts they have developed during the course to demonstrate that they have understood the process of gathering and evaluating information (see Appendix 8.2).

Regardless of whether learning will actually be formally assessed your planning should involve thinking about whether and how assessment could be usefully measured. The ultimate assessment is of course the student's successful completion of the their university studies.

Dealing with disasters

Teaching disasters do happen; it is inevitable. There are however things you can do to help ensure that you minimise the chances of disasters. Lessons plans and teaching programmes should not be set in stone; you have to be flexible. For example, imagine the following scenario: you arrive to teach a postgraduate masters class assuming they will have a basic knowledge of IL. You then discover, after talking to them, that the majority are international students and have no IL skills at all. You have a choice: you can plough on regardless, or you can change your plan and adapt the session appropriately. If you stay with the planned session you will probably confuse them and put them off asking you for help in the future. The sensible thing is to adapt your session. This is not always easy to do, especially if you do not have a lot of teaching experience, but don't be afraid to take five minutes out to scribble down a new timetable for your session. Online courses are particularly useful in this situation as they allow for adaptation and change. For instance:

- you can give some units to the students as homework and then ask them to complete a quiz, based on these units at the following session;
- assessment – self-test can be changed to quizzes and vice versa;
- units within VLEs can be hidden so that students can not see them before you use them for teaching.

If you are not using an online course then have a memory stick or a CD with all your presentations and worksheets on it. This way, if you have the above scenario you can quickly swap to a presentation intended for first year undergraduates that would be more appropriate for the situation. You can also ask for new worksheets to be printed off and photocopied. Remember to talk to your academic contact and inform them of the situation, they may be able to give you additional time to help the students. Always be prepared for things to change; be adaptable and flexible!

If you are planning a hands-on session with databases, remember that at the beginning of term every other university is doing the same. This can lead to problems with students accessing the databases. Always have online tutorials/worksheets for several databases; this way you can switch if required. It is better to have them doing something rather than nothing!

Top Tips: avoiding disaster

Planning ahead is the best way to minimise potential disasters. Here are some useful tips:

- Make sure you know your teaching material, and have had a chance to rehearse your session. This will help you with timings, and should highlight any problems before the session – much better than finding them during it!

- If two or more people are running the session, it is very helpful to do a run-through, as again this helps with timings, and you can ensure each person knows which section they are responsible for. Arrange who will do the preliminary announcements and introduction, and any summing up.

- Save your presentation(s) to a memory stick and CD.

- If you haven't used the room you'll be teaching in before, arrange a visit so you can check the layout and find out what extras you may need to take.

- Check that the equipment works and that you have the correct cables and other connections.

- If you are using a PC room that normally has student access, print out notices for the doors of the room where you are teaching, and have blu-tack/sellotape with which to stick up notices. This will help prevent unwanted disturbances from people wandering in to use the computers.

Top Tip continued

- Have a list of the library and, where possible, local IT contacts, including phone numbers.

- If you are using an online programme and it requires a student login, make sure you have generic passwords, as there will always be at least one student who can't log in!

- If using Athens passwords, take a list of training passwords as there will always be someone who doesn't have theirs with them.

- If you are using printed worksheets or handouts, ensure you have enough for the class.

- Evaluation is important, so ensure that you have enough feedback sheets for the class.

- If you are using a VLE with hidden units, make sure you have 'activated' all parts of your course that you will need for teaching. Any quizzes you use will also need to be set according to the dates you want it to be available to students.

- If the worst comes to the worst and nothing works, don't be afraid to cut your losses and stop the session.

Adapted from: *iLIP – Internal Information Literacy Programme* (Imperial College London, 2005).

Coffee and petit fours

The success of your meal can usually be judged by the time you reach the coffee and petit fours. If people are relaxed and smiling it usually means they are content and happy. Similarly, if your students are interacting with you, asking you questions, it usually means they have found your session interesting and useful. Evaluation however, is essential. You must evaluate how successful your IL programme or session has been for your students. It is very important that you look at your own performance as a teacher, and at the tools you are using to teach with. You should always question and learn from every session, as this allows you to develop your own teaching and the tools you use. You may wish to find out different types of information depending on type of student you are teaching, so you may have a selection of different evaluation sheets. When designing your evaluation sheets always start with thinking about what you really want to know, then design the questions around this.

Always hand out an evaluation sheets at the end of the course and, if possible, hold focus groups with students – particularly if you are using an online course, as you can discuss design, navigation etc. in the discussion too. An example of an evaluation sheet can be found in Appendix 8.3 at the end of this chapter.

Cake and champagne

The importance of sharing your experiences of teaching IL cannot be overstated, and those of us lucky enough to work in teams should talk with colleagues on a regular basis and share good practice. The best way to learn is from each other and peer observation can provide a variety of helpful ideas and boost our confidence. An ideal way to manage peer observation and take away some of the stress of feeling watched is to team teach. For many of us it is the size of groups that limits what we feel we can comfortably achieve, so working in twos will benefit both the students and ourselves. Whenever possible, ask academic tutors to work with you, and don't be afraid to ask them to comment on particular aspects of your teaching. It is important to remember that one very possible reason why academics shy away from working with librarians is that they have very little confidence in their own information literacy.

Top Tip

> When you are teaching, keep a reflective journal. Fill it in after every teaching session and refer back to it when planning any future teaching sessions.

Conclusions

The aim of this chapter was to look in some detail at IL in the higher education sector. If you are new to teaching in higher education, then we hope the chapter will help you get started. Don't forget, if you have colleagues who are more experienced then ask for their advice and use their knowledge to help you. Keep in touch with what is happening in IL in HE by joining an e-mail discussion list, such as lis-infoliteracy at JISCmail, or set up a Google Alert. If you are an experienced teacher, we hope this chapter has given you some new ideas or ways of improving what you do. It is essential to keep on evaluating your teaching and looking for new and innovative approaches to take into the classroom. Whether you are creating a picnic or a banquet you need to plan carefully. By planning your meal, knowing who your guests are, the types of ingredients required, and selecting an appropriate methodology, you can help to ensure that you have a successful meal that everyone will enjoy. By doing this you will also feel confident about what you are serving and you will enjoy the meal too!

References

Boden, D. and Holloway, S. (2004) 'Learning about plagiarism through information literacy: a fusion of subject and information management teaching at Imperial College London'. Proceedings of the JISC Plagiarism: Prevention, Practice and Policies Conference.

Bruce, C. (1997) *Seven Faces of Information Literacy*. Adelaide: Auslib Press.

Bruce, H. and Lampson, M. (2002) 'Information professionals as agents for information literacy', *Education for Information*, 20(2): 81–106.

Buckley Owen, T. (2003) 'Lessons in information literacy', *Information World Review*, 191: 24.

CILIP (2006) 'Information literacy: definition', available at *http://www.cilip.org.uk/professionalguidance/informationliteracy/definition/* (accessed 8 February 2007).

Conole, G. and Oliver, M. (eds) (2007) *Contemporary Perspectives in e-Learning Research: Themes, Methods and Impact on Practice*. London: Routledge.

EDULIB Project (1998) *Teaching for Learning in Libraries and Information Services: a Series of Educational Development Workshops*. Hull: Centre for Teaching and Learning Support, University of Hull; Dundee: University of Abertay, Dundee.

Eisenberg, M. and Berkowitz, B. (2007) 'The Big 6', available at *http://www.big6.com/* (accessed 8 February 2007).

JISC (2006) 'eLib: The Electronic Libraries Programme', available at *http://www.ukoln.ac.uk/services/elib/* (accessed 8 February 2007).

JISC (2005) 'i-Skills publications', available at *http://www.jisc.ac.uk/publications/publications/pub_sissdocs.aspx* (accessed 8 February 2007).

JISC (1998) 'EduLib: educational development for higher education library staff', available at *http://www.ukoln.ac.uk/services/elib/projects/edulib/* (accessed 8 February 2007).

Joint Funding Council's Libraries Review Group (1993) *The Follett Report*. Bristol: HEFCE; available at *http://www.ukoln.ac.uk/services/papers/follett/report/* (accessed 8 February 2007).

Lave, J. and Wenger, E. (1991) *Situated Learning: Legitimate Peripheral Participation*. Cambridge: University of Cambridge Press.

Levy, P. and Roberts, S. (eds) (2005) *Developing the New Learning Environment: the Changing Role of the Academic Librarian*. London: Facet Publishing.

Manchester Metropolitan University (2004) 'The Big Blue', available at *http://www.library.mmu.ac.uk/bigblue/* (accessed 8 February 2007).

MLA (Museums, Libraries and Archives Council) (2004) 'Inspiring learning for all', available at *http://www.inspiringlearningforall.gov.uk/* (accessed 8 February 2007).

Nankivell, C. and Shoolbred, M. (1995). *Presenting Information*. London: Library Association Publishing.

National Committee of Inquiry Into Higher Education (NCIHE) (1997) *Higher Education in the Learning Society (Dearing Report)*. London: The Stationery Office.

Norman, J. (ed.) (1998) *South Wind in the Kitchen: the Best of Elizabeth David*. Harmondsworth: Penguin.

Oxford Brookes University: Oxford Centre For Staff And Learning Development (2007) 'Learning theories', available at *http://www.brookes.ac.uk /services/ocsd/2_learntch/theories.html* (accessed 11 February 2007).

Ramsden, P. (2003) *Learning to Teach in Higher Education*, 2nd edn. London: RoutledgeFalmer.

Rossett, A., Douglis, F. and Frazee, R.V. (2003) 'Strategies for building blended learning', available at *http://www.learningcircuits.org/2003/jul2003 /rossett.htm* (accessed 8 February 2006).

Rusbridge, C. (1998) 'Towards the hybrid library', *D-Lib Magazine*, July/August; available at *http://dlib.ukoln.ac.uk/dlib/july98/rusbridge /07rusbridge.html* (accessed 13 April 2007).

Secker, J. (2004) *Electronic Resources in the Virtual Learning Environment: a Guide for Librarians*. Oxford: Chandos Publishing.

SCONUL (Society of College, National and University Libraries) (1999) 'Information skills in higher education: briefing paper', available at *http://www.sconul.ac.uk/groups/information_literacy/sp/papers/Seven_pillars 2.pdf* (accessed 8 February 2007).

SCONUL (Society of College, National and University Libraries) (2006) 'The seven pillars of information literacy', available at *http://www.sconul.ac.uk /groups/information_literacy/sp/seven_pillars.html* (accessed 8 February 2007).

Smith, M.K. (2003) '"Communities of practice", the encyclopedia of informal education', available at *http://www.infed.org/biblio/communities_of_pratice. htm* (accessed 19 February 2006).

thebigblue (2002) *'thebigblue' Final Report*. July 2002. Available at *http://www.leeds.ac.uk/bigblue/* (accessed 24 February 2007).

Watkins, C. (2003) *Learning: a Sense-Maker's Guide*. London: Association of Teachers and Lecturers.

Webb, J. and Powis, C. (2004) *Teaching Information Skills: Theory And Practice*. London: Facet Publishing.

Webber, S. and Johnston, B. (2005) 'UK academics' conceptions of, and pedagogy for, information literacy', available at *http://dis.shef.ac.uk /literacy/project/about.html* (accesssed 8 February 2007).

Wenger, E. (1999) *Communities of Practice. Learning, Meaning and Identity*. Cambridge: Cambridge University Press.

Appendix 8.1

Example lesson plan

Session Leader:

Session title: Invisible Library

| Date: | Time: | Length of session: | No of students |

Learning outcomes:

Students will develop:
- £ familiarisation with the different types of information the library provides and how to access them;
- £ an ability to create a search strategy and apply Boolean logic, wildcards, truncation etc;
- £ familiarisation with chosen database.

How will you know the learning outcomes have been reached by the students:
Self tests students will complete in OLIVIA Units 2 and 4.
The hands-on online tutorial session will uncover any problems students may be having; help can be given at a point of need.
Online evaluation form to be completed before end of session.

Assessment:
Formative assessment – self tests

Additional notes:
Homework – ask them to work through the Metalib Informs tutorial

---

Activity	Student or lecturer	Content	Timing
Presentation	Lecturer	Information resources, search techniques	15 minutes
Demonstration	Lecturer	Demo of WoK (or relevant database) Do basic search show results, how to print/save, SFX button, etc	10 minutes
Hands-on	Student	Look through OLIVIA online Units 2 and 4. Complete self-tests Work through database online tutorial in OLIVIA Unit 4	30 minutes

Appendix 8.2

Critical evaluation assessment form

Name: _____

Course: _____

What is your project topic? _____

- Is the information you have retrieved relevant to your assignment and does it answer the whole question?
- What keywords have you used for your search?
- Which synonyms and alternative spellings have you identified for each of your key terms?
- Have you remained focused on your keywords throughout your search or did you get distracted and go off at a tangent?

Is the information up to date?

- How many references have you retrieved?
- What is the publication date range of the items used and how did you decide this is appropriate?
- Did you use the publication date limit appropriately, if available?

Are you confident your information was produced by a reputable source?

- Which resources have you used and why are they appropriate for your search?
- How have you assessed that the information has come from a reputable source?
- Is any of your information peer reviewed? If yes, give an example.
- Have you used information from the Internet and if so how have you assessed the quality of the information?

How do you know that the information is of an appropriate academic level?

Appendix 8.3

UG Evaluation Sheet

Your name (Optional): ....

Your Course: ....

Date:..

Location:..

.

Session Name:............................(you add in)...........................

Tutor(s) Name:.......................... (you add in)...........................

Key
5 – Excellent, 4 – Very good 3 – Good, 2 – Adequate , 1 – Not very good

- Did you find this session useful?

5 4 3 2 1

- What have you learnt from this session?

....

- Where do you think you could apply what you have learnt today to the rest of your course?

....

- How useful did you find this online course when learning about Information Literacy?

....

- Which units did you find most useful?

....

- How useful did you find the:
Online Tutorials	5 4 3 2 1
Self-Tests	5 4 3 2 1

Quizzes   5 4 3 2 1
Critical Analysis Sheets   5 4 3 2 1

- Were there any topics not included that you would have liked to have seen covered?

....

- Please rate the quality of your tutor

Tutor   5 4 3 2 1

- How do you fine rate the quality of the venue?

5 4 3 2 1

- Do you have any comments/suggestions that would help us improve the programme?

....

9

Conclusion: coffee, cheese, biscuits and petit fours

Jane Secker, Debbi Boden and Gwyneth Price

The end of a meal is a time to relax, to feel the appetite pleasantly sated and enjoy a sense of wellbeing. For the cook, it will be a good time to consider her successes and reflect on ways to perfect the recipes next time or create a more balanced meal. Our conclusion will consider some the ideas and issues raised by the individual chapters in this book and present an overview of practical issues in information literacy (IL) in 2007.

Reflecting on preparation

After the event it is all too easy to recognise how lack of preparation has marred the meal. It is useful to reflect on the kinds of education and training we might consider essential for all librarians, whether they work in public libraries, specialist institutions or Education.

Twenty-first century librarians need to be outgoing people, they need to like people and empathise with the learning needs of their users, so they need to understand what learning is and what it might be. Working at the Enquiry Desk, or answering enquiries by phone or e-mail, will call on the Librarian's own understanding of information and its uses, so a Librarian must be information literate. Although the concept of 'the information-literate librarian' seems an obvious one it is surprising how unprepared library staff often are for this aspect of their work. New online IL programmes have been developed to help fill this skills gap. Pop-i (which is mentioned in Rónán O'Beirne's chapter) was piloted in 2006 with Bradford Metropolitan Council and phase two of the project is LolliPop. This project is a collaboration between Bradford College, Imperial College London and the universities of Bedfordshire and Loughborough. LolliPop aims to develop library staff's IL skills and enable them to transfer these skills into the workplace.

A scientific approach to cooking

In a recent article on Heston Blumenthal, the three Michelin starred chef, Dr Peter Barham is quoted as saying 'He realised that understanding what he was doing in the kitchen might actually help to make life easier' (Hickman, 2005). Librarians cannot stand still and make assumptions about the ways in which information is found and explored; we must keep in touch and get involved with research. For librarians in HE there are increasing opportunities to be researchers as well as practitioners, and practitioner research has led the way in the development of how we conceive of the information-literate student or academic. For librarians in other sectors opportunities are fewer, particularly for those working alone or in under-funded services. We hope the chapters in this book demonstrate some of the synergies between library sectors and may suggest further areas for cross-sectoral practitioner research. Relationships between Education sectors are obvious, Moira Bent's current work on School to University transition (Moira's infolit blog can be found at *http://blogs.ncl.ac.uk/moira.bent*) will prove useful, but perhaps the relationships between work place and other sectors are less obvious areas for exploration. Annemaree Lloyd's study of the information literacy of firefighters (Lloyd, 2005), for example, throws some fascinating light on one of HE librarians' obsessions, the apparent failure of academics to engage with information literacy.

Planning the menu

This book was primarily conceived as a book for librarians who teach (or train); for us as academic librarians those roles are clear, but our authors have demonstrated throughout this book that our 'users' are not so easily organised.

If we are to develop a menu that will appeal to all our guests we have to know their likes, dislikes and preferences, the size of their appetites and anything that might prevent full enjoyment of the meal. Whichever library sector we work in, this is extremely difficult to do. On a one-to-one basis, we should use all our skills as questioners to help our client, when we are working with large groups we are very dependent on the group leader, often a teacher or lecturer. Concern over the difficulties of working with others is not new; in 1984 Norman Beswick wrote:

> The skills of a cook are important, but, as Mrs Beeton told us, before cooking one's hare, it is important to catch it. Until we have articulated to our teaching colleagues why the library is important to them in everything that they do, it may well be that we are standing in the kitchen before we have done our shopping. (Beswick, 1984)

When we plan our menu, we need to have a clear picture of the finished meal, the learning outcomes. This is never easy – our cookbook does not have photos of the finished product to help us predict how delicious the meal will look. In reality the learning outcomes may be different for each learner and there is no final result as no one is finally and completely information literate; it is an ongoing, lifelong learning experience. The complexity of information literacy is only beginning to be recognised and we are moving beyond a skills agenda. We need much more research to unravel how to go about 'Untangling spaghetti' in IL learning and teaching (Williams and Wavell, 2006).

The future

The future for teaching librarians is exciting and challenging and we can learn many lessons from the ways in which attitudes to food and cooking have changed over the last few years. Like fast food, Google has become a vital part of many people's lives, but an increasing number of people are more web savvy and more sophisticated in their eating habits. Librarians, now more than ever, must play their part in providing opportunities for all, both to narrow the digital divide and to widen horizons.

The Alexandria Proclamation of November 2005 recognised the fundamental importance of IL, stating:

> Information Literacy lies at the core of lifelong learning. It empowers people in all walks of life to seek, evaluate, use and create information effectively to achieve their personal, social, occupational and educational goals. It is a basic human right in a digital world and promotes social inclusion of all nations. (IFLA, 2005)

As our world becomes increasingly digital, so the ability to navigate the information environment becomes crucial to our survival. Information literacy must be recognised as distinct from IT literacy, but inextricably linked to it. The ubiquitous nature of technology, from mobile phones, to handheld gaming devices, from satellite navigation in our cars to wi-fi access in our leisure spaces and places of work means that technology surrounds us, but must not come to dominate us.

It is difficult to predict how technology might develop over the next 10 years, but what is apparent is that it will become easier to use and an even more important part of our daily lives. We are already awash with information, just as a large supermarket presents us with more food and choices than we could ever hope to eat, so the Internet and digital world can easily overwhelm us. This is why, just as good nutrition and basic cookery skills should be taught from an early age, so information literacy should become embedded into the curriculum of schools, universities and provided as additional support and training throughout life. Web 2.0 or the rise of social networking technologies is currently being heralded as a revolution, with individuals as not just consumers of information but providers. Log in and add your comments to 'Trip Advisor', sign up to 'MySpace' to meet new friends, share your photos on 'Flickr' and share your videos on 'YouTube'. This is the age of the amateur information provider, but in fact it means information literacy is more pertinentand already we see critiques of *Wikipedia* featuring in IL education. If anyone can contribute, we must be sure we can separate the wheat from the chaff.

A final note is to ask that we reflect on our future role in this fast and developing digital world. At present we are still debating whether we should be using the term information literacy or information fluency, others suggest academic literacy and so the debate goes on. What we call it, does not really matter, it's how we interact with our users, be it in a formal classroom, at a PC or at that enquiry desk that counts. We also have the other literacies such as media, digital and e literacy. There is considerable overlap between all of these and yet, we tend to exist in our own silos with our own agendas. The global information society should be an exciting place for the information profession as long as we step forward and grasp the opportunity. We should break out of our silos and collaborate with those working in areas with overlap; together we have the ingredients to create a banquet with dishes to tempt, educate and scintillate the tastebuds, but alone we have bubble without the squeak!

References

Beswick, N.W. (1984) 'The School Library: what should we tell the teachers?' *School Librarian*, 32(1): 13–18.

Hickman, L. (2005) 'Doctor food', *Guardian Unlimited*, April 20; available at *http://www.guardian.co.uk/food/Story/0,2763,1463749,00.html*

Lloyd, A. (2005) 'Information literacy: different contexts, different concepts, different truths?' *Journal of Librarianship and Information Science*, 37(2): 82–8.

Williams, D. and Wavell, C. (2006) 'Untangling spaghetti? The complexity of developing information literacy in secondary school students'. Scottish Government; available at *http://www.scotland.gov.uk/Resource/Doc/930/0040947.pdf*

Index

Printed in the United States
102905LV00001B/181/A